FLIGHT OF THE BLUE HERON

Book given.

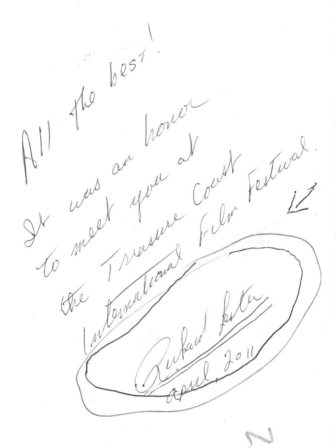

All the best!
It was an honor
to meet you at
the Treasure Coast
International Film Festival.

Richard Foster
April, 2011

FLIGHT OF THE BLUE HERON

Stories of a Lifetime

BY

RICHARD LESTER

www.BookstandPublishing.com

Published by
Bookstand Publishing
Morgan Hill, CA 95037

2946_3

978-1-58909-662-2

Printed in the United States of America

PREFACE

Imagine all the people living life in peace. You may say I'm a dreamer, but I'm not the only one. I hope someday you'll join us, and the world will live as one.

John Lennon

People want peace so much that, one of these days, governments had better get out of the way and let them have it.

Dwight D. Eisenhower

ACKNOWLEDGEMENTS

This book is dedicated to the heroic Zabinski Family of Warsaw, Poland — Jan, Antonina, Ryszard, and Teresa.

Their love for both people and animals had no limits.

———

The author also dedicates this work to Armin D. Lehmann. At age 17, Armin found the road to peace, compassion, and tolerance.

He followed that road faithfully throughout his adult life.

———

Finally, a word of deep gratitude to my family — Ann, Amber, and Gary. Their support of all my projects, and their patience with me, have known no limits.

This labor of love is especially for them.

Contents

	Preface	v
	Acknowledgements	vi
I.	The Journey Begins	1
II.	The Range Rider and Marshal Dillon	3
III.	A President is Assassinated	7
IV.	The Ku Klux Klan Had a Machine Gun	9
V.	My New Friend, Mary	13
VI.	Cruising With The Byrds	15
VII.	Joe Meets The Beatles	19
VIII.	Karl, the Gestapo Officer	23
IX.	Anne Frank's Diary and Peter's Cat	29
X.	The Lawman's Son	33
XI.	Billy The Kid Died Confused	37
XII.	Pat Garrett is Bushwhacked	43
XIII.	Another Sheriff, Another Mystery	47
XIV.	Bullet Holes in the Walls	57
XV.	A Tail Gunner Named Bob	61
XVI.	The Marine Ace	67
XVII.	Courtney's Story	71
XVIII.	Courier of Peace	75
XIX.	Armin Becomes a Peacemaker	79
XX.	Claire Goes into Hiding	83
XXI.	Safe Haven at The Warsaw Zoo	89
XXII.	A Reign of Terror	97
XXIII.	Israel's Blue Heron	109
XXIV.	The Zookeeper's Son	113
XXV.	Global Dreamers	121
XXVI.	Walking in Beauty	125
XXVII.	Fuzzy Little People	129
XXVIII.	Charlie and Dottie	133
XXIX.	Starring Miss Scarlet	137
XXX.	The Man with the Handlebar Moustache	139
XXXI.	Batman's Sidekick	147
XXXII.	My Son, Gary	151
	Reflective Thought	161
	About the Author	162

I

The Journey Begins

If you want others to be happy, practice compassion. If you want to be happy, practice compassion.

Dalai Lama

Why is it that we seldom reflect back on our journey through life until we find ourselves approaching our twilight years? From our earliest days as children, we experience a wealth of important moments which produce every human emotion possible.

Our memories are of past triumphs and tragedies — events which have produced great joy, as well as great sorrow. Those moments from the past have been both serious and humorous. They are — taken in their entirety — what compose our unique time on planet earth.

What is it that causes us in our twilight years to reflect back on what has been? Is it possible that we simply have come to realize that we have a story which must be told to future generations?

I can't speak for others, but I personally have come to believe that my life has been shaped and influenced by some incredible people. Every one of them has a story worth telling. I have spent a lifetime listening to the experiences of others. I have learned that the world is filled with amazing people who — more often than not — are eager to tell their personal stories to someone who is willing to take the time to listen.

I have been an exceptional listener all of my life. At various times, I have shared some of the stories I have heard. In 1980, at the age of 35, I wrote up my first story in a popular monthly magazine. It was a tale about a crime-busting sheriff in Tennessee who became a national hero, only to lose his life under questionable circumstances.

Twenty-five years passed, and it wasn't until 2005, that I began telling stories on a regular basis. That was the year I formed a small film production company — Blue Heron Films — in order to provide a platform for my son Gary to launch his first documentary production.

When I discovered a company in Georgia also producing documentaries under the same name, I changed the name of our company to Blue Heron International Pictures. Within five years, Blue Heron had access to more incredible stories than my son or I could ever tell. The few that we did publicly share on film influenced and changed our lives forever.

As our documentaries soared to breathtaking heights of acceptance throughout the world, I began to realize that heroes and villains are with us at every stage of our journey through life.

Even before Blue Heron took wing, I had stories to tell. Perhaps my first encounter with a hero was when I was eight years old.

II

The Range Rider and Marshal Dillon

The year was 1953. I had been born with crossed eyes, and I was headed for the hospital for corrective surgery. On the way, my Dad stopped at a shopping center. It was there that I met my first TV hero — The Range Rider, (otherwise known as Jock Mahoney).

There he was — standing in a shopping center parking lot, all dressed up in his western outfit. The real Range Rider was actually signing autographs for all the kids. A solid mass of boys my age led their fathers by the hand to where the Range Rider was signing those precious autographs.

I was in awe. There he was. Just like he looked on our small black-and-white TV screen. The real Range Rider! Like many of the other kids, I didn't have the courage to talk to him, but I sure did want his autograph.

Dad scrounged a scrap of paper from the glove compartment of our new Chevy Bel Air, and I approached the actual, living, breathing, in-person Range Rider himself.

I handed my western hero the paper, watched him write something on it, and eagerly reached out to retrieve it. I could see that the scrap of paper now had a large signature scrawled on it: 'Range Rider.'

Would you believe that almost sixty years later, I can still visualize that signature in my mind? It was one of those moments of a lifetime. Within minutes of meeting my hero, it was off to the hospital and corrective eye surgery.

Two years later, I still found most of my heroes coming from the black-and-white television screen. Every day, I faithfully tuned in to Buffalo Bob Smith and his puppet pal, Howdy Doody. I waited patiently for Kate Smith to finish singing *When The Moon Comes Over The Mountain* on her daily variety show.

I believe it was scheduled right before my show came on, but I'm no longer sure. In my mind, I can still hear her beautiful voice, however, and picture her friendly smiling face, as she sang her popular theme song.

I do remember watching the tail end of Kookla, Fran and Ollie during some of those early childhood years also. In any event, it was always a thrill when Buffalo Bob Smith came up on the television screen with that clarion call, "Hey kids, what time is it?" To which everyone in the Peanut Gallery — and some of us in the home audience, as well — responded, "It's Howdy Doody Time!"

On Saturdays, I was up early so as not to miss Roy Rogers and especially Sky King. Sixty years later, I still recall the Sky Bar candy commercials that allowed actor Kirby Grant to fly his plane across the family TV screen, accompanied by his niece, Penney.

Then there were the nights I got to stay up a little later to watch Marshal Matt Dillon. He protected the citizens of Dodge from the various scoundrels who found their way to Kansas during each exciting episode of *Gunsmoke.*

I liked the quiet way Marshal Dillon spoke, as well as the fact that he was a man of few words. I also liked his fast draw at the beginning of every episode. When he couldn't disarm the bad guys with reason, then his six-gun did the talking!

As a young teenager, I briefly explored the possibility of becoming a fast-draw artist myself. Marshal Dillon definitely had an early influence on me.

III

A President is Assassinated

By the 1960's, my collection of heroes was changing. At 15, I engaged in politics for the first time, and handed out campaign literature for John F. Kennedy. I recall distributing a small, glossy pamphlet outlining his thoughts about education.

As I look at some of those fliers today, I can't help thinking how fast the sands of time flow through the hourglass. Three years after JFK was elected president, I was a freshman in college. His assassination had such a profound impact on me, that I still remember exactly what I was doing in my dorm room, when someone shouted out the horrific news in the hallway. It was hard to comprehend the fact that someone had killed the president. That had never happened before in my lifetime.

When an opportunity came up to attend JFK's funeral services at Arlington National Cemetery, I jumped at the chance. Two college buddies and I felt it was such a momentous event, that we just had to be there to personally experience history in the making. We hitch-hiked to Washington, DC and took our place among all who had come to mourn.

While we were standing outside the church in Washington, waiting for the funeral cortege to pass by, a ripple went through the crowd. Lee Harvey Oswald, the alleged assassin, had himself been shot dead by a man named Jack Ruby. It was electrifying news, and the crowd seemed unable to comprehend the meaning of it all.

As the vehicle carrying family members passed by, I saw little John-John in a blue suit, sitting on someone's lap (I believe it was a Secret Service agent). He was staring out the car window at those of us who formed the curbside crowd. He too seemed unable to fully comprehend it all.

Later on at Arlington, I was moved by the fly-over with one jet missing from the formation. I was amazed at how Charles de Gaulle, leading the group of dignitaries, towered over everyone beside and behind him. My eyes were focused mainly on the Kennedy family, however — Bobby, Ted, Jackie, Carolyn, and John-John.

As for De Gaulle, I didn't know much about him. For sure, he was the president of France, resplendent in his brown uniform and kepi cap. My only impression at the time, however, was that he was an extremely tall person. He towered over the people around him — much like my western hero Marshal Matt Dillon (played by James Arness, by the way), who I remember seeing in person at the Illinois State Fair when I was about nine years old.

IV

The Ku Klux Klan Had a Machine Gun

Peace is not merely a distant goal that we seek, but a means by which we arrive at that goal.

Martin Luther King, Jr.

My college days were spent in a small, sleepy southern town. My college was proud of its liberal philosophy, having admitted one black student to the student body. He kept quietly in the background and out of the public eye during the entire time I was there. Looking back at those times, I believe it took courage for him to be on that southern campus, and courage for the college administrators to admit him.

The 1960's were very turbulent times, although they didn't impress me as such at the time. Those were the days when members of the Ku Klux Klan lived and worked among us, and you never really knew if someone might be connected to the Klan.

KKK rallies were held in the rural areas of the south. Working part-time as a radio newsman, I actually attended one of those rallies, stationing myself near a car packed with FBI agents.

At the rally, white-robed Klan leaders claimed they had a machine-gun if outsiders tried to interfere. They sang some kind of country music, but the songs were filled with words of hate and intolerance.

9

The speaker encouraged everyone to stay calm throughout the meeting. "We have a machine-gun," he announced, in case outsiders were to arrive and try to disrupt the proceedings. To emphasize that they meant business, the KKK burned a cross at the end of the rally.

What I found extremely amusing about the one and only Klan rally I ever attended, was how many seedy characters in bib coveralls came by the FBI car where I had positioned myself. Each one gave an oral report to one of the federal agents. At one time during the rally, I began to think there were more FBI informers in attendance than there were true Klan members.

In my college, race relations never really became a hot-button issue. The war in Viet Nam was what really occupied our minds. Would we even make it through college before getting drafted?

When I first arrived on campus, I joined the Army ROTC unit and dreamed about becoming an officer. Before the end of my freshman year, however, I learned that ROTC graduates from my college were being assigned as forward artillery observers. Artillery observers were sustaining a very high casualty rate in the jungles of Southeast Asia.

I decided to drop out of ROTC, and began working on a teaching credential. My goal was to land an occupational deferment from the war (It worked, by the way. I was never drafted, and stayed in education most of my life).

I never understood why we sent so many members of my generation to their deaths in a war that never had any purposeful meaning — at least to those of us who tried to make any sense out of it.

V

My New Friend, Mary

Some people — like flowers — give pleasure just by being.

Anonymous

One of the smartest decisions I made as a college freshman was to join the staff of the college radio station. Everyone wanted to be an announcer, and no one wanted to be the Director of Classical Music. When I learned that the classical music director merited a small office in the performing arts building (which housed the radio and television operations), I had no problem making my decision. I would learn about classical music on the job, and be the only freshman on campus with a private office.

Within a year, I was working part-time for the commercial radio station in town, and helping promote college concerts. That's how I managed to spend two hours talking to Mary Travers of Peter, Paul & Mary.

Mary was the sweetest person I ever met on campus. For two hours, we talked about everything under the sun, including the fact that her husband Barry Feinstein did the album cover photography for the group.

Mary shared her fear of flying, a fear which probably had its roots in the recent memory of Buddy Holly, the Big Bopper, Richie Valens and the fatal plane crash that abruptly ended their promising musical careers.

Then, suddenly, it was time to go on stage. Mary had used our conversation to chase away pre-performance butterflies, and she ended our chat with, "I live just a few doors down from Ethel Merman's apartment in Manhattan. If you are ever in New York, be sure to drop by."

Within minutes, she was on stage belting out, "If you miss the train I'm on, then you will know that I am gone…"

VI

Cruising with The Byrds

Perhaps the most unusual people I met during those radio and concert promotion days, were a group of singers calling themselves 'The Byrds.' They had a number of hit songs at the time, including *Turn, Turn, Turn* and *Mr. Tambourine Man*.

It was Saturday night. Shortly before 10 PM, their concert wrapped up. We ushered the performers to our vehicles and drove them to the local Holiday Inn. After awhile, I checked on them to make sure their rooms were to their satisfaction.

As I walked in one of the rooms, they were all there — jumping up and down on the beds like little kids. Jim McGuinn, the lead singer who wore the trademark granny glasses, asked where we could go to get some food. I had to remind him that he was in a sleepy southern town where they rolled up the sidewalks by 9 o'clock each night, and Saturday was no exception.

Then, the first zany plan I ever hatched in my life popped into my brain. I told McGuinn that if he and the group would pile into my vintage Oldsmobile, go to the local burger joint with me, and offer autographs and a tip, we might be able to persuade the teenaged crew to cook up a last batch of burgers and fries.

Rather than look at me like a crazy man, the group thought the plan sounded great. They stopped jumping on the motel room beds, ran out the door, and piled into my car.

Sure enough, I met resistance at the burger place. As I tapped on the window, the surly teenager cleaning the grill shouted, "We're closed!"

"I don't think so," I shouted back. "Just take a look at who's in my car. They'll sign autographs for you and give you a generous tip."

I had the kid's attention. Nothing like this had ever happened in his 16 years of life. What type of idiot would try to re-open a burger joint after it had closed, he must have wondered. Then the kid looked out and saw the famous face with the granny glasses, sitting in my car and looking back at him from the rolled-down rear window.

"Holy, cow! It's the Byrds!!!" Other employees rushed to the store window. McGuinn and his fellow musicians took it all in, looking at the crew quietly from inside the car. The grills went back on, the take-out window opened back up, and the teenagers on duty at the burger joint that night got a story they could tell their family and friends for a lifetime.

The Byrds got their burgers and fries. The burger crew got their autographs (and actually met the group member who went up to the window to help me carry the food back. I forget who it was, but I think it was Jim McGuinn, since he was the most recognizable face in the group.)

I also forget what the group ordered to drink. After all, it was more than 40 years ago.

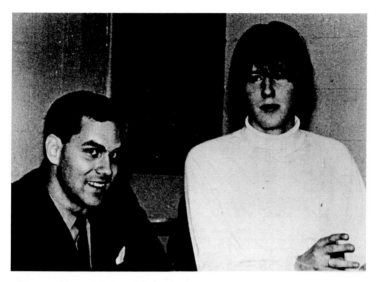

The author with Byrds' drummer Mike Clarke before burgers

VII

Joe Meets The Beatles

With the successful outcome of the 'Byrds and Burgers' adventure, I learned one of those valuable lessons in life — lessons which present themselves occasionally. I knew that I could think outside the box, apply a creative solution, and remove an obstacle in the path leading to a successful conclusion. It wasn't long before my wild and wacky side kicked back in, and the target in my sights was none other than an immensely popular mop-haired musical group from England — The Beatles!

When I first learned that the world's most famous performers were coming to the United States, I was working as a school-teacher, earning little more than a hundred dollars a week. I supplemented my income with my part-time radio job, which I had started back in my college days.

There was that wild and wacky side of the brain kicking in again. I knew that an American movie director living in England worked on a Beatles movie called *Help*. It just so happened that his name was Richard Lester also. My actual name is Richard Lester, Jr. I wondered if I could use my name to accomplish the impossible: a personal meeting with the Beatles.

I typed up a brief letter to Tony Barrow in England, who was handling all press relations for the group. I simply said that I planned on being in New York the same time 'the boys' were, and that I would need clearance to drop in on them. Then I signed the note 'Richard Lester, Jr.'

I have no idea what went through Tony Barrow's mind. I do know that he fired an immediate letter back to me, saying the group was presently on tour in the Far East, and he would have Bernice Young in New York arrange for the passes and credentials I would need. It looked like I was soon going to be visiting with the world's most famous performing group.

Sure enough, I heard from Bernice Young in no time. I had the credentials I needed in order to go right into the Beatles' private rooms at the Hotel Warwick in New York City.

I had originally intended to share my second set of credentials with a good friend. Gene Loving was the afternoon DJ at the local radio station where I was working as a part-time newscaster. I read the news, he spun the platters, and together we 'ripped the wraps off the stacks of wax' and created the number one sound in town.

However, Gene was unable to take time off from work, so I boarded my flight to New York with two sets of credentials. Then, as luck would have it, I ran into a friend from town. We'll call him Joe. Joe, if you reading this, you already know that this next wacky adventure is one in which you became the main star.

Joe was a family man with a wife, a couple of kids, and a steady job. I forget how we met, but we sure came from opposite ends of the spectrum. I was single, adventurous, and did whatever seemed like fun at the moment. Joe was quiet, steady-going, and a real rock of security for his family.

However, at that particular time, life had dealt Joe one of its complicated wrinkles. After a series of disagreements with his wife, Joe decided to hop a plane, take a brief time-out, and visit his mother up north for a few days. As luck would have it, Joe ended up on the same flight as mine.

I asked Joe what his plans were after arriving in New York. He told me his story, and I said, "Joe, I have just the thing to take your mind off the marital problems."

As I explained the significance behind my second set of credentials, Joe's eyes widened, and I believe he made the first-ever decision to do something wild. He agreed to accompany me into the Beatles' hotel room!

Once we visited with Ringo and George for awhile, all of us moved into an adjoining larger room where the *Fab Four* were going to hold a press conference. Joe and I took our seats in the front row and the conference began.

Since this was a hotel room, not a conference room, seats were limited. There was room for network cameras, but not all of the reporters that usually went with them.

So the TV news organizations had to rely on others to ask the questions. At one point, Joe raised his hand and asked a bombshell of a question. I don't recall what he asked, but I do know that all three networks had their cameras rolling.

Once the conference was over, we bid goodbye to the world's most famous entertainers and exited the Hotel Warwick. At a nearby restaurant, we sat down for a couple drinks, and Joe had an epiphany. He realized that his disagreement with his wife was not worth the time away from his family. He decided to return home, but first he would call his kids and tell them about his marvelous adventure.

When his son got on the line, Joe told him he had just been with the Beatles. His son responded, "I know Daddy. We just saw you on Walter Cronkite!"

I believe Joe did visit his mother briefly before returning home to an anxiously awaiting family. His personal story had a happy ending, and all was forgiven by the time Joe arrived back home — a newly minted celebrity from the CBS Evening News With Walter Cronkite.

To this day, I believe in the power of a name and the doors it can open. Yes, I did visit with the Beatles, spending most of the time with Ringo Starr and George Harrison. Those two were definitely the most down-to-earth of the foursome. Ringo blew smoke rings with his cigarillo for the benefit of my camera, and George invited me to visit him at his home on my next trip to London (as if school-teachers with part-time radio jobs could even think of hopping a jet to London!)

The only raised eyebrows occurred when I met manager Brian Epstein. He recognized the name. Did he wonder about the connection? I'll never know. I had my photos. I had my day with the Beatles. Joe was back home with his wife and kids. Life was good.

VIII

Karl, the Gestapo Officer

"Those who cannot remember the past are condemned to repeat it."

George Santayana

Before my radio days finally came to an end some twenty years after they started, I had met a veritable *Who's Who* of the contemporary music world. Sam the Sham told me he regretted not going to college before his number one hit song *Woolly Bully* made him an overnight sensation. Jimi Hendrix shared some quiet backstage time with his stunning Danish girl-friend, showing a personal side totally opposite the mad-man style of his on-stage persona.

The Beach Boys seemed to enjoy recording promos for my radio show. These were the glory days of rock and roll, and I was right there with the people who shaped the sounds of the era. I loved my part-time radio job. My students were also glad I had these opportunities. They never knew whose photographs I would bring to class next.

By the end of the 1960's, a subtle change in interests started occurring — a change I didn't notice at first. I was starting to develop more of an interest in history, than in contemporary rock-and-roll music.

On three different occasions, I headed off to Europe with the idea of researching and writing a book about the Hitler Youth. At the time, not much existed in print about

23

the group, and I thought I might be the one who would write the break-through book.

What actually happened is this. I came back with so much material that I had no idea how to even begin to organize it. The project drowned in an avalanche of unorganized and disorganized notes that became impossible for me to even begin to deal with.

I did, however, come across one memorable character who definitely did *not* become one of my heroes along the way. He may not totally fit into the nasty villain niche either. I don't know. I think it may be most accurate to say that this individual caused mixed feelings in those who knew him, were victimized by him, or heard his story.

When I first made contact with Karl Silberbauer, he was working in the foreign identification bureau of the Vienna police department in Austria. I have no idea what his duties were, but assume he somehow kept track of foreigners — like me.

Karl had mixed feelings about sharing his story with an American radio reporter doing research for a book. I do remember agreeing not to use anything he said in my Hitler Youth book. I was young and naïve, with no journalistic experience whatsoever. I was happy just to get his story, so I agreed. No publicity. Nothing in print. He would remain 'on background.'

Karl's story began on August 4, 1944. He was the equivalent of a plainclothes detective (Oberscharfuehrer) in the Gestapo, when his supervisor — Julius Dettmann — dispatched him to Prinsengracht 263 in Amsterdam, Holland.

Silberbauer arrived at a nondescript warehouse with several Dutch detectives in tow. The local Gestapo office had a telephone tip from 'a reliable source' that Jews were hiding there.

Miep Gies was working in the front office. Around 11 AM, she recalled a short man in plainclothes suddenly opening her office door and brandishing a pistol. Meanwhile, Karl Silberbauer entered Victor Kugler's office and started asking about hiding places in the warehouse.

It was only a matter of time, before the raiding party discovered a staircase with an entry-way hidden behind a bookcase. That day, Karl Silberbauer arrested Hermann van Pels, Auguste van Pels, Peter van Pels, Fritz Pfeffer, and one of the most famous names to emerge from the Holocaust — Anne Frank. He also took into custody her sister Margot, mother Edith, and father Otto Frank. Kugler and his associate Johannes Kleiman were arrested for harboring Jews.

While his name will live in infamy because of this event, I do not believe Karl Silberbauer was inherently evil. He definitely did not seem to be a rabid Nazi. Otto Frank himself refused to help Simon Wiesenthal make a case against Silberbauer after the war, claiming Silberbauer treated him and his family with respect. Frank suggested that the real villain to be pursued was the informer who gave them all away.

The fact that Miep Gies lived to tell her side of the story as one of Anne Frank's principal rescuers, also speaks to the issue of Silberbauer's lack of total dedication to his job. When Miep mentioned to him that she noticed he had a

Viennese accent and that she too was from Vienna, Silberbauer calmed down and did not arrest or detain her — despite the fact that she was obviously guilty of crimes that could warrant the death penalty. Had his superiors found out about this, Silberbauer's career would have been over, and he would at best be on his way to the Russian Front.

Silberbauer told me that after the war he contacted Otto Frank and asked for his forgiveness. Silberbauer also told me that Frank had indeed forgiven him for his part in the raid.

My mistake, which I regret to this day, is not contacting Otto Frank to confirm what Silberbauer was telling me. I tend to think, but can never prove, that it was true.

In subsequent writings, Otto Frank did confirm that he and Silberbauer actually sat down for a short conversation during the raid. It did seem to bother Silberbauer to have to arrest a man who he discovered held an Iron Cross from the first world war. He asked Frank why he did not somehow safely remove his family from the reach of the Third Reich before it came to such a desperate situation.

Early in life, Karl Silberbauer had become a policeman in Vienna, like his father before him. In 1939, he joined the Gestapo and moved to the Netherlands. In 1943, he transferred to the Sicherheistdienst in The Hague. After the war, he eventually found his way back to the Vienna police department, where I found him.

Silberbauer shared his story with me when he was in his late 50's. He had just bought all new furniture on time payments, and lived in fear of losing his job. Anne Frank's diary had been turned into a book, a Broadway play, and even a Hollywood motion picture. People throughout the world were beginning to connect with this 14 year old, who came so close to becoming just another anonymous victim of the Holocaust.

Silberbauer was worried about the growing public awareness. He wanted to make it perfectly clear to me that he was a policeman following orders, and to do otherwise was to risk prison or death (which he did anyways, regarding Miep Gies).

Silberbauer claimed Anne Frank looked very much like her photos, only older and prettier. Then he dealt me the remark of the century. In one sentence, he showed me his total lack of understanding as to who the victims of the story really were. He said, "If I knew then what I know now, I would have burned that book!" For Karl Silberbauer, former Gestapo officer, Anne Frank was the inconvenience that could cost him his furniture and his job.

Interestingly, Miep Gies, who arguably owes her life to him, also admits that — had she known what was in the diary — she too would have burned it. It contained far too much dangerous information about them all.

As we know now, no one burned Anne Frank's diary, and her voice will always be a reminder of man's inhumanity to his fellow man.

Karl Silberbauer died at age 61, a few years after sharing his story with me. During the Holocaust, he chose to hurt more people than he helped, and history will have to decide whether Karl Silberbauer is to be forgiven by others beyond Otto Frank.

IX

Anne Frank's Diary and Peter's Cat

The best remedy for those who are afraid, lonely, or unhappy is to go outside — somewhere where they can be quiet, alone with the heavens, nature, and God. I firmly believe that nature brings solace in all troubles.

Anne Frank

My first exposure to the Holocaust came around 1959 when I was the only 9th-grader cast in the high school play. It was also my first step into the world of the performing arts.

I have forgotten many of the names associated with that time in my life, but I can still picture Catherine Wormley, the director, who gave me my first chance to be an actor. Mrs. Wormley planted the seeds that would cause a life-long love affair with theater, film, and the entertainment world in general.

The play was *The Diary of Anne Frank*. I vividly recall much of my experience portraying Dr Dussel, the dentist who provided the comic relief in the play with his numerous disagreements with Anne.

Everything else connected with my days at Colonie Central High School in Albany, NY is long forgotten. I still can picture the soft-spoken Mrs. Wormley, however, and all my fellow cast members — just as if it were yesterday.

Back then, I had never heard of Karl Silberbauer, with whom I would be in contact in Austria ten years later. I didn't know that my character's real name was Fritz Pfeffer, and I gave little thought to the immensity of the Holocaust, other than the fact that most of this particular group of people were sent to a concentration camp where they died.

At the time, I had a friend named Wayne who lived across the street. His dad had something to do with film distribution to theaters, and I recall his dad arranged a special screening of the 20th Century Fox movie version of the story for me and Wayne. This would be my first special screening of a motion picture.

One last thought before we leave the Anne Frank story. History frequently overlooks many random acts of kindness, and there is one detail of Anne's story that I do not believe has ever been published.

In researching the material for this book, I discovered the fate of Mushi, a cat belonging to Anne's boyfriend Peter. Anne mentions Mushi in her diary, and Mushi appears in both the play and the movie. What happened to the real Mushi? No one has ever said.

Animal lovers are found throughout the world, and Amsterdam, Holland in 1944 was no exception. Once the raiding party had departed Prinsengracht 263 with their prisoners, the building was again quiet. Mushi remained in the annex for awhile, but it was evident that he clearly missed Peter. Eventually, a cleaning lady took him home, where she cared for him the rest of his life. Peter's beloved pet was safe. Peter, however, would perish in a concentration camp.

After my experience with Karl Silberbauer, almost 40 years passed before I took another look at the Holocaust. In between, I was about to become enthralled by the exploits of a couple of legendary sheriffs.

The first one killed Billy The Kid.

X

The Lawman's Son

All of my life, I have held to the belief that everyone has a story to tell. I have been especially fond of seeking out senior citizens in their 70's and 80's. That seems to be a stage in life where people are reaching out to everyone and anyone who will take the time to listen to what they have to say.

In the mid 1980's, I came across a tall, lanky gentleman living in a small apartment in Albuquerque, New Mexico. He was almost 80 years old at the time, and seemed to be in excellent health. He enjoyed golfing, but preferred that I do the driving when we were together. His name was Jarvis P. Garrett, and — believe it or not — he was the youngest son of Sheriff Pat Garrett, one of the most famous lawmen in the history of the wild west.

"In some of my travels, people didn't believe that I was the son of Pat Garrett," said Jarvis. "So I carried this birth certificate, which was filled out by the father back then. It shows that I was his son and not his grandson. See how he filled out the certificate himself — with his signature there?"

Jarvis handed me the old document, and sure enough — there was the famous "Pat F. Garrett" signature at the bottom right. The famous lawman's handwriting filled in all of the blanks on the official document.

Jarvis told me he was two-and-a-half years old when his father was murdered in 1908. Most of what he would share with me had been handed down to him from his mother. She told him the stories his dad shared with her.

When his mother started telling Jarvis all of the family stories, he was a teenager working as an usher in the early movie theaters of the day. His only recollection of his father's death was a few vague memories of the wake that was held in the family home back in 1908.

Jarvis' impressions of his father most certainly were shaped by his mother years later. "My dad was a quiet, handsome man." said Jarvis. "He was six feet four and a half inches tall, very slender, and he moved with a cat-like rhythm. He was quite a dancer."

Jarvis had no use for any of the Hollywood movies about Billy The Kid and his dad. In fact, he was a bit distressed that people would glamorize an outlaw, but forget about the courageous lawman who brought the outlaw to frontier justice.

"In 1930, there was a movie, *Billy The Kid* (starring Johnny Mack Brown as The Kid). Wallace Beery portrayed my father. Beery was short, squat, and fat. In the movie, tobacco juice spilled from his mouth. My father was actually tall and slender," recalled Jarvis. "Then, in 1943, Howard Hughes made *The Outlaw*, starring Jane Russell. It also had no resemblance to any historical fact."

According to Jarvis, Hollywood never got it right. "The stories were just ridiculous."

Then Jarvis dropped a bombshell. "In 1958, they did a film called *Left Handed Gun*, starring Paul Newman as The Kid. The real Billy the Kid *wasn't even left-handed!"*

I was working at the time as a school principal and invited Jarvis to come speak to my students. He agreed, if I would do the driving. So I picked him up at his apartment, and we headed out for my school, where he enthralled the kids with his story of Billy The Kid's sudden demise. Jarvis also shared insights about his father's murder in 1908.

I still have his recorded narrative to this day, as riveting now as it was 25 years ago.

Jarvis Garrett

XI

Billy the Kid Died Confused

When Lincoln County Deputy Sheriff John Poe told his boss that Billy the Kid might be holed up in Fort Sumner, Sheriff Pat Garrett thought the idea had very little merit. The gossip of the day had the Kid hiding in Old Mexico. For The Kid to actually be hiding right under the New Mexico lawmen's noses, was unthinkable.

Nevertheless, Poe told Garrett that while he was in White Oaks, a source he trusted brought a message from Pete Maxwell in Fort Sumner. The source allegedly claimed that Maxwell was irate over the fact that the Kid was starting to look with favor on Maxwell's sister, Paulita. According to writer Leon Metz, the Kid was also said to be romancing a local girl named Celsa Gutierrez, whose husband Zaval apparently didn't mind.

Jarvis wasn't so sure about this romantic tidbit. "Celsa Gutierrez was actually my mother's sister. She was blonde and blue-eyed, taking after my grandmother," recalled Jarvis, adding another hidden nugget of truth to the history books.

It does seem a bit far-fetched to me also that a ruthless outlaw, as some historians contend, would romance the sister-in-law of the man-hunter who was pursuing him. I wonder how many of those historians knew of Celsa's family ties to Pat Garrett and his son Jarvis.

Whatever the ultimate reason, Pat Garrett half-heartedly decided to check out Fort Sumner. Just for good measure, he and Poe rode to Roswell to pick up a third man-hunter — Thomas L. "Tip" McKinney. McKinney also thought the idea of The Kid hiding in Fort Sumner was a long-shot, but he agreed to go along for the ride.

On the night of July 10, 1880, Sheriff Pat Garrett and his two man posse rode into the history books. Three nights later, they reached the hills about six miles outside of Fort Sumner. Garrett was still convinced he was on a wild goose chase, but decided to stake out the Gutierrez residence, which was a part of the quartermaster's office on the former military post.

Hiding in a nearby peach orchard, the lawmen almost stumbled on a young couple romancing on the ground. The two were speaking softly in Spanish, not unusual since Fort Sumner was mostly composed of Mexicans and only about a half dozen Anglos. Within minutes, both lovers were gone. I wonder who it was that the Garrett posse observed in the peach orchard that night.

A festival with music and dancing was going full swing in town that night, so the lawmen stayed clear of Fort Sumner. Strangers were sure to be noticed.

Around midnight, Pat Garrett decided to drop in on Pete Maxwell to see what he knew. Nothing was going on at the peach orchard, now that the young lovers had departed.

The lawmen soon arrived at Maxwell's place, a one story adobe building with a porch surrounding three sides. The front door to Pete's bedroom was standing open, in order to allow whatever breeze might be blowing to come in and cool down the inside.

As Pat Garrett stepped into the darkened bedroom, his deputies lounged outside. McKinney found a spot near the picket fence, while Poe stationed himself near the edge of the porch. There was no sign of Billy The Kid, nor did they really expect to find any. Inside the darkened bedroom, Garrett gently awakened Pete Maxwell, and then sat down to have a chat.

A short time before, Billy the Kid, who had been enjoying the fiesta in town at the Garcia home, decided to head back to the sheep camp where he lived in hiding. For some unexplained reason, he turned his horse around and headed back to town.

Billy stopped in on his friend Bob Campbell and told Campbell he was hungry. Bob tossed him a knife and told Billy there was a side of beef hanging off of Pete Maxwell's porch.

Garrett's deputies saw him coming, but they didn't recognize him. Because they were convinced at this point that their quarry was nowhere around, the deputies simply stayed quietly in place, alert but not alarmed.

The Kid wasn't expecting to find lawmen on Pete Maxwell's porch either. He was right there on top of them before he realized they were there. "Quien es? Quien es?" he called out, assuming they were a couple of locals lounging around. The Kid pulled out his pistol. Things began to spiral downhill from there.

Tip McKinney started to stand up, caught his spur on a porch board, and almost fell over. That's when Billy the Kid discovered these two guys on the porch were armed. He sprinted down the porch and backed into the open door leading to Pete Maxwell's darkened bedroom.

Before Maxwell or Garrett had time to react, Billy The Kid was inside the bedroom. "I often think of Pete Maxwell," said Jarvis. "That was an awful predicament for him to find himself in."

Garrett was sitting on Maxwell's bed.

"He had no sooner sat down on Mr. Maxwell's bed when this man entered the room with a knife in one hand and a gun in the other," recalled Jarvis. "He almost touched my father's knee, and then he moved back when he realized that there was a third person in the room."

Pete whispered to Garrett, "That's him." To Garrett's consternation, his holster had slipped behind his back and was not easily accessible. Then Billy The Kid made his last fatal mistake. It was a big one. With gun drawn, he hesitated to shoot. Instead, he called out, "Quien es? Quien es?" "Who is it? Who is it?"

Pat Garrett had not been idle in those few seconds. By now, he had worked his holster around to where he could pull out his pistol with the seven inch barrel.

"My father leaned to his side, expecting to be shot, but hoping to only be wounded," recalled Jarvis. Pat Garrett's revolver roared with a blinding flash, and roared again. "My father was lucky. For the first time in his life,

The Kid hesitated. That hesitation cost him his life," Jarvis concluded.

At that point, Maxwell and Garrett ran out of the room, knocking down John Poe.

According to Jarvis, "My father saved Pete's life by yelling not to shoot, that it was Pete."

When Poe heard Garrett's account of the shooting, he panicked. The last place in the world he expected to meet up with Billy The Kid was at the Maxwell house. "Pat, you killed the wrong man," he exclaimed.

Garrett and Maxwell were sure it was The Kid, but no one knew if he were dead. He might have only been wounded — or even unharmed — and waiting in ambush for them to return to the room. Poe and Maxwell claimed to hear a death rattle, however.

Locating a candle, Garrett peered into the window and saw The Kid lying on the floor, the butcher knife in one hand and his revolver in the other. "The first shot killed him. The second shot hit a washstand," Jarvis remembered.

Why did Billy The Kid hesitate that fateful night? Pat Garrett told his wife (who told Jarvis) that he believed The Kid thought the other man in Maxwell's bedroom was a friend named Manuel Abreu, one of Pete Maxwell's Mexican friends.

Abreu was a local rancher who The Kid also knew. Since Garrett was seated, his tall height didn't betray him. Mistaken identity and hesitation made the difference between who lived and who died that fateful night.

XII

Pat Garrett is Bushwhacked

Pat Garrett also died by the gun. His murder remains a mystery to this day. One man confessed to killing him, and was even arrested and tried for the crime. Yet hardly anyone believes he did it, including Jarvis Garrett. Historians have several versions of the event, and Jarvis had his favorite theory also, based on the information he gleaned from his mother.

Here's what we know. On Friday afternoon, February 28, 1908, Carl Adamson rented a buggy in Las Cruces, New Mexico. He headed north on the four hour drive to the Garrett ranch. Adamson's relative by marriage, James P. Miller, had offered Garrett a business deal which would solve his growing financial problems.

The deal also involved a local sheep-rancher named Wayne Brazel. Adamson arrived at the Garrett ranch that afternoon, and Pat Garrett showed him around. The next day, the two set out for Las Cruces, with Garrett in the driver's seat of the buggy.

Jarvis' mother told him that Adamson made a bad impression on her. He was a short, stout fellow who made her feel nervous and suspicious. She expressed her concerns to her husband before he left, but he paid no attention to her.

"My mother was very apprehensive," recalled Jarvis. "Around noon, a gust of wind blew our house door closed, and Mother said she believed something had happened to my father."

Perhaps Mrs. Garrett's strong negative first impressions, which she conveyed years later to Jarvis, were a major factor in his conclusion that Adamson — if not his father's actual killer — was at least deeply involved in the murder plot.

At the time I knew Jarvis, he told me he had run into New Mexico Congressman Joe Skeen, Adamson's grandson. Jarvis told Skeen, "Your grandfather killed my father." Skeen allegedly replied, "Nah, he wouldn't have done a thing like that!"

In any event, when the buggy reached Alameda Arroyo, Adamson was driving. He pulled over to urinate, and Garrett also climbed down to relieve himself. By this time, Wayne Brazel had joined them on horseback. Before Garrett finished urinating, two shots rang out, and the legendary sheriff fell over dead — shot from behind.

Historians over the years believe Jim Miller was lying in wait that day, and that Carl Adamson stopped at a pre-arranged place. Miller, a man with between 20 to 40 contract murders to his credit, actually pulled the trigger. It turns out that he earned his living as a hired assassin. As I mentioned before, Jarvis and the Garrett family believed Adamson was the trigger-man, however, not Miller.

The one man who actually confessed to killing Pat Garrett is the person no-one believes actually did it. Wayne Brazel admitted that he killed Pat Garrett. He was arrested for the murder and tried for it. In a trial which could only be considered a travesty of justice, Brazel pleaded self-defense.

Despite the fact that the victim was shot from behind while urinating, the jury felt self-defense was as good a story as any. So they acquitted Brazel.

"My father was shot in the back of the head, with the bullet coming out over the right eye," said Jarvis. "I went out to the murder site in 1956 with an old friend of my father's. He showed me where it actually happened, and mentioned that my father had a shotgun, but it was in a case on the buggy unopened. It sure wasn't self defense, but out and out murder."

In his well-written book, *Pat Garrett: The Story of a Western Lawman*, Leon Metz asserts that there were really five suspects in the murder plot. In addition to Miller, Adamson, and Brazel, he also identifies ranchers W.W. Cox and Print Rhodes.

Jarvis contributed information to Metz for his book, and read it when it was published. He would continue to maintain that Carl Adamson was the actual trigger man, but that he did not act alone. "No question, my Dad's death was a plot," said Jarvis. "There were some very prominent people involved. They met in an El Paso hotel and made plans to kill my daddy. "

Jarvis doesn't mention Print Rhodes, but adds two other names to the group of alleged conspirators: local rancher Oliver Lee, and none other than a man who would become Secretary of the Interior under President Warren Harding. His name was Albert B. Fall. History best remembers him for his involvement in The Teapot Dome scandal. Jarvis believed he also had blood on his hands connected with Pat Garrett's murder.

On my last visit to Jarvis' apartment, I remember him sitting on his couch beneath a huge oil painting of his dad. With a twinkle in his eye, Jarvis asked me, "See that little treasure chest over there? Want to see what's in it?" Would anyone in their right mind have said no?

Jarvis handed me the box and I opened the lid. "I didn't even show this to Leon Metz," he said with a smile.

Inside were all that was left of the famous lawman's effects. I picked up and read Pat F. Garrett's life insurance policy from the New York Life Insurance Company. In plain view was his neatly written signature on the policy.

Then Jarvis pulled out his own birth certificate, with another clear *Pat F. Garrett* signature written carefully in black ink. "Back in those days, the father had to sign the birth certificates," said Jarvis.

I had hoped one day to go out to the site of his father's murder with Jarvis. As a young man, his father's friends had taken him there and showed it to him. However, much to my regret, I never took the time, and before I knew it, Jarvis Garrett had passed away. With him went an oral history originating with Sheriff Pat Garrett, as told to his wife, and eventually to Jarvis.

I remember Jarvis as a quiet, gentle soul. He had a quick and easy smile, and a great sense of humor. Jarvis was definitely a distinguished and likeable gentleman. It was hard to believe that murder formed a part of his childhood memories.

XIII

Another Sheriff, Another Mystery

I find it quite a coincidence that my travels through life would bring me into contact with not one — but two — law enforcement officers who died under mysterious circumstances.

This chapter contains graphic violence that may not be suitable for younger readers. I ask that parents read it first, and then decide how it should be presented. I sincerely believe, however, it is a story that must be told, and told accurately in every detail. It takes place in August, 1967.

When the phone started ringing shortly before 4:30 in the morning, McNary County Sheriff Bufford Pusser had only been in bed for about an hour-and-a-half. "There's some trouble down near Hollis Jourdan's place," he told his wife Pauline, who had also been awakened by the call. "Buford, I want to go with you," she replied.

Pauline Pusser knew her husband very well. He was an extremely dedicated Tennessee lawman. In the course of his career, he had been shot eight times and stabbed seven. A fleeing moon-shiner even clipped him with a car. It was no wonder that Pauline worried about her husband. In fact, ever since he had been involved in a fatal gun-battle at the state line, he had been receiving threatening phone calls.

Pauline found them unnerving. "Buford, I want to go with you."

Buford Pusser knew that something else was on his wife's mind. Today was the day they needed to start packing for a trip to rural Haysi, Virginia to visit her parents. He knew Pauline would be nervous about him staying out on patrol all day long. Buford agreed to let his wife ride along.

Slipping into a white blouse, dark brown slacks, and black loafers, Pauline picked up a country music cassette and followed the McNary County sheriff to his patrol car. While Buford checked his .41 magnum and glanced at the automatic shotgun next to his knee, Pauline loaded the tape into the cassette player below the dash.

The lawman's late model Plymouth was soon roaring down the country road at 100 mph. As it approached New Hope Church, the conversation centered around tomorrow's trip to Virginia.

Buford never saw the dark colored Cadillac until it was directly behind him and about to pass him. At that moment, his heart started to pound. His law enforcement instincts started to kick in. There was no legitimate reason for someone else to be barreling down that winding country road at such excessive speeds.

That was probably his only thought before a blaze of gunfire erupted. Much later, Pusser would recall that he saw three men in the Cadillac — two in front and one in the back. The passenger in the front seat was the one who opened fire with a 30 caliber rifle. Pauline had been hit and was slumped in the front seat, but Buford's first thought

48

was to take evasive action and get away from the deadly gunfire.

When Pauline started to make some gurgling sounds, he pulled the riddled patrol car over to tend to his stricken wife. Out of nowhere, the gunmen reappeared, opening fire again.

Buford Pusser was no stranger to pain. He had broken his back in three places, required 192 stitches after a particularly vicious stabbing, and had been beaten by pipes and wrenches. Not to mention being shot. Nothing in his past, however, prepared him for this.

As the patrol car windows disintegrated into a thousand shards of glass, Buford Pusser felt the left side of his face fly off in a torrent of blood. Later on, doctors would find that the shots blew away all of his lower teeth and the gums on the left side of his mouth. Part of his tongue was missing, and what was once the skin of his left cheek now hung in tatters down his neck.

Before he could begin to recover from this violent trauma, a bullet tore into Pauline's head. Buford saw the top of her head fly out the passenger window, while both lobes of her brain spilled into his lap. The patrol car was drenched in blood. Everything was crimson red.

As unbelievable as it sounds, Sheriff Buford Pusser did the unthinkable. He put the patrol car in gear and raced after the fleeing killers. However, his wounds were so grave, that he would soon have to pull over. He passed out from loss of blood, and that is how his deputy — Pete Plunk — found him.

At the time, Buford Pusser didn't know it, but he was about to become a national hero, lionized in a series of films by Bing Crosby Productions. It will always be a source of great pride for me to know that I had a small part in creating that legend.

A few years after his death, I wrote an article about Buford Pusser for *True Detective* magazine. Bing Crosby Productions found Pusser's death an interesting subject also. However, when *Walking Tall: Final Chapter* was eventually released, I only recognized factual material in the last six or seven minutes of the film. The rest, in my opinion, was pure Hollywood baloney!

For years after my magazine article was published, I remained in contact with both his mother, Helen Pusser, and his deputy and close friend, Pete "Peatie' Plunk. I never intended to write a magazine article, so the story behind the magazine article is also worth telling.

It was during the Viet Nam War era, and I was working as a school teacher, which — as I mentioned earlier — conveniently provided a deferment from the draft. I was just starting to collect autographs, and had gone to see a movie called *Walking Tall*. That summer, I planned on a vacation which would take me right through Tennessee, where Helen Pusser and Buford's daughter still lived.

I called Mrs. Pusser on the phone, told her how much I appreciated her son's story, and asked if she would send me her autograph. She responded with an invitation to drop by the family home. I wasted no time in accepting the invitation.

I arrived at the neat and attractive brick home in Adamsville, Tennessee with the idea of visiting for an hour at most. As it turned out, my visit lasted three days (That home is now a museum open to the public).

Mrs. Pusser showed me Buford's personal belongings, including all of his grade school report cards — which she still treasured as his mother. She introduced me to his brother, Big John, who operated a furniture store in town. I also met his deputy, Pete Plunk, who was working as a car salesman (Even that many years later, Pete wore a pistol in an ankle holster for protection).

Pete generously offered to take me around to all of the actual locations where the Buford Pusser story occurred (The original movie, I discovered, was filmed in a nearby county and not on the actual locations in McNary County). Pete and I visited the motel where Pusser was involved in a fatal shootout — complete with bullet holes still in the wall. I also visited New Hope Church, behind which the killers were waiting that fateful August morning.

We ended our tour with Pete taking me to the crash site, where the life of the legendary sheriff ended a few years after the horrific ambush. By the time I arrived back at the Pusser home, I had a huge number of details concerning what really happened to Buford Pusser. Much of my information was far different from the story that would eventually be told by Hollywood.

Then the moment occurred that would link me to the Buford Pusser legend forever. Mrs. Pusser handed me the tie rod from her son's red Chevy Corvette — the vehicle he crashed and died in a few years earlier.

The tie rod was in two pieces. Mrs. Pusser pointed out the surface where the tie rod had been split. She told me there was no way it could have snapped at impact with a dirt embankment during the fatal crash. Pete Plunk agreed.

"The skid marks tell me that Buford did the only thing he could do — lock the car down and brake his speed, because he couldn't turn his wheel. If the tie rod were to fall off your car, you would automatically hit the brakes and lock it down," said the former deputy.

Mrs. Pusser told me that a few days before her son's fatal accident, the car was not in his possession. It was in a garage getting some mechanical work done.

She believed that during that time, someone partially sawed the tie rod, weakening it to the point that it broke, as Buford was returning home from a night at the county fair. He lost control of his speeding vehicle and crashed into a dirt embankment. The car flipped and caught fire. The legendary sheriff from *Walking Tall* was dead.

The highway patrol ruled it an accident. Mrs. Pusser and Pete Plunk believed otherwise. The tie rod could be just the piece of evidence that would point to murder. After all, who would believe that a man trained in high speed pursuit would lose control of his vehicle under normal driving conditions, and not try to steer out of the situation?

Besides, Buford Pusser was a guy who pursued his wife's killers while he himself was gravely wounded. He didn't lose control of his bullet-ridden patrol car, and he continued to pursue the shooters as he slipped into shock. Buford gave up only when he found himself slipping into unconsciousness.

Now everyone was expected to believe that he froze at the wheel of his car on a familiar road, under normal driving conditions, while coming home from the county fair. It just didn't seem plausible.

There was also some concern about his behavior the weekend before the fatal crash. Buford certainly had some high medical bills from all of the reconstructive surgery that was necessary to put his face back together. However, there had been two films and some substantial money coming in from Bing Crosby Productions — far more than the medical bills required. Where was it? Buford wanted to know.

That weekend, he went around town telling people that someone close to him was taking his money, and he intended to find out who it was. No one doubted that he would do what he said he would do.

Then Buford Pusser was dead, the family believed that movie money was missing, and the tie rod looked suspicious. I agreed to contact a friend of mine who worked for ABC radio in Washington. He alerted the producers of the network's television news shows. It didn't take long for the producers to report back that they weren't interested. The Buford Pusser story was just too old.

Meanwhile, Mrs. Pusser reported to me that she had been contacted by someone who claimed they could get the story on those very same news programs. She sent him the tie rod, and he soon disappeared, along with the only piece of crash evidence still in existence (To this date, neither he — nor the tie rod — have ever been located).

Years later, the Ku Klux Klan tried to mount an invasion of the tiny island of Grenada. The federal government disrupted the plot, and — according to one of my sources — some of the financing for the madcap scheme may have been none other than the 'missing' Buford Pusser movie money.

Buford might have been right, after all. Someone could have been taking his money for their own purposes, and he believed it had to be someone close to him — someone he trusted.

I wondered what I was going to do with the mountain of material I had collected about Buford. I kept thinking about a very disappointed old lady back in Tennessee, who had lost both her son and her daughter-in-law. Her grandchildren were orphans. She was hoping against hope that someone would shine the public spotlight on her son's suspicious death.

Then I got a break. I was reading the classifieds in *Writer's Digest* and noticed that *True Detective* magazine was in the market for some interesting stories. I knew that *True Detective* was the publication that first brought the Pusser story to the attention of Hollywood. So I contacted the editor, told him what I had, and asked if he were interested in me writing the story.

Al Govoni, the chief editor, got back to me in no time. Yes, he absolutely wanted the story. No, it wasn't too old — not for the magazine that first brought public acclaim to Sheriff Buford Pusser.

So Al gave me the green light, and he personally guided me through the experience of writing my first national magazine article. When it was completed, Al called me and asked me to expand my story into a double feature. It would get the cover. I would be paid double, and he would also pay me for every photo that ran with the article, whether it came from me or the magazine's files.

Most important of all, I was about to debut as a national magazine writer for a publication that went back to the 1920's. I was excited for myself and for Helen Pusser, who would now get her version of the accident out in print.

Al Govoni was a heck of a nice guy. I have had a number of mentors in my life, but Al stands tall as my inspiration in magazine writing. He even let me try my hand at writing the sidebar piece, which was usually the editor's territory.

The rest is history. *True Detective* published 'Buford Pusser's Last Ride: Accident or Murder?' Al Govoni told me the issue sold out, and they only had an archival copy left. I also know that he generously shared his last few copies with the magazine's biggest fan — Mrs. Helen Pusser in Adamsville, Tennessee.

Buford Pusser with his mother, Helen

XIV

Bullet Holes in the Walls

I have no doubt that Buford Pusser dealt with some pretty rough customers in his life-time. How rough? Let's look at the shoot-out in the motel room that I visited with Pete Plunk, where the bullet holes were still visible in the walls.

Louise Hathcock operated the Shamrock Motel in McNary County, right near the Tennessee-Mississippi state line. Her boyfriend, Towhead White, ran the White Iris Café across the street. Bed and board were not the only services that the couple provided. Most of their income came from illegal alcohol, prostitution, and gambling. They did far more than offer out-of-town travelers a night's rest and barbecue ribs.

Greed knows no limits, and Louise and Towhead never seemed to be able to rake in illegal money fast enough. So they cooked up a plan that eventually led the Triple A Auto Club to designate that route between Chicago and New Orleans as one of the most dangerous in America.

Unlike Motel 6 at night, Louise left the Shamrock's light on only for so long. Then, under the cover of darkness, Towhead would come over. The pair would enter sleeping tourists' rooms, where Towhead would hammer the innocent travelers to death while they were asleep in their beds. After removing their wallets and valuables, he and Louise would dump the victims' bodies in the river.

A few of the Shamrock's guests were far more fortunate. Some tourists were separated from their money through strong-arm tactics and intimidation, but were allowed to live. Pete Plunk believed the Tennessee River has still not yielded up all of the bodies of those who fared far worse, however.

The murder and mayhem went on for quite awhile. Pusser finally was able to get arrest warrants for Louise on illegal whiskey and theft charges. As he and deputies Pete Plunk and Jim Moffett arrived at the motel, they found Louise in an ugly mood. She had a bourbon and coke in her hand.

Then Sheriff Pusser hit pay-dirt. Louise decided she wanted to come clean and give him all the information he needed about her illegal activities. She had one condition. Only he could go into her living quarters, located just off of the motel office. The deputies had to wait in the lobby.

Pusser agreed. Then things went downhill in a heartbeat. Louise opened a dresser drawer and pulled out a .38 caliber revolver. Buford Pusser fell against the door in an effort to get out of her line of fire. Louise fired off a round that plowed harmlessly into the plaster near the sheriff's head. She ran toward him, attempting to fire a second time, but the gun misfired.

By now, Pusser's .41 magnum was in play, and he fired at Louise. The first shot hit her in the neck. So did the second shot. His final round went into her jaw and she was dead before she hit the floor. Her bourbon and Coke remained unscathed on the dresser.

As for fame and fortune, *Walking Tall: Part 1* grossed 70 million dollars. Buford Pusser received three residual checks for $155,419. His mother died believing she knew who was behind his murder, but without the satisfaction of ever having it proven.

XV

A Tail Gunner Named Bob

War is cruelty, and you cannot refine it.

General William T. Sherman

George Caron liked to be called Bob. I can't remember how I first came across Bob, but it had to be in the late 1980's or early 1990's. He lived with his family in Denver at the time. One of the interests I hoped my son Gary would pick up as a hobby was collecting autographs. So I am sure that is how my relationship first began with Bob Caron.

Bob was the tail gunner on the Enola Gay for the atomic mission over Hiroshima. One of the most widely publicized photos of the crew has Bob kneeling in front, wearing a Brooklyn Dodgers baseball cap.

Bob always expressed the hope that no one in the future would ever witness what he had seen from the tail of the Enola Gay. When we knew Bob, we were living in a place he remembered very well — Roswell, New Mexico.

It was in Roswell on November 20, 1945 that Bob received his discharge from the military. His wife Kay had driven to Roswell from Dodge City, Kansas to pick him up. When she saw how skinny he was — only 115 pounds at the time — she told him not to worry, because her mother's home cooking (especially the fried chicken) would fatten him back up.

When I first met Bob, he still loved to fly, and was proud of his membership in the Confederate Air Force, an organization that restored and flew the old warplanes. As a memento, I remember him sending Gary one of his CAF membership cards, and I still have photos he had taken toward the end of his life as a passenger in one of the old war-birds.

Before he boarded the Enola Gay and flew off into the history books, Bob Caron was just an ordinary GI. I particularly like the story he told about the time he spent in Florida. He was part of the B-29 Accelerated Service Testing Group, but he didn't recall if the outfit even had a number.

It was definitely a very special outfit. Apparently, the unit was designed to attract very little attention, and had become almost invisible to the military bureaucracy. Bob remembers that they were always about three months behind in getting their pay. One thing they did get was plenty of flight time — seven days a week, all day long.

The pilot, Colonel Paul Tibbetts, took special care of his men, however. He knew they would be asked to do what no one throughout all time had ever been asked to do. So, Tibbetts grew a bit concerned one day when General Wolfe, head of the 58th wing, cancelled a Christmas leave that he had previously promised to Tibbetts' men.

Instead of flying to Atlanta to celebrate the holiday, the crew would again be up in the skies over Florida, doing what they did all day — day in and day out. Christmas leave in Georgia was cancelled.

Christmas Eve, 1944 arrived, and Bob recalls that he was in the mess hall, after a busy day working on the plane. The crew chief came running in and shouted to the guys to get their shaving kits and Class A uniforms. They were going to Atlanta after all.

Bob was the first one to arrive at the plane. Tibbetts was standing there. "What's up, Colonel? How come we're going to Atlanta?" he asked. With a grim look on his face, Tibbetts replied, "We have to go in for repairs."

Bob looked at the plane and could detect nothing amiss. Tibbetts then said, "Look up there. We have a tear in the rudder."

Bob had to look hard before he spotted the tiniest tear that could easily have been fixed within minutes — right there on the field. "You're not afraid to fly with that tear are you?" Tibbetts asked, with a gleam in his eye. He seemed barely able to stifle a laugh.

"Colonel," said Bob, "If it means getting to Atlanta for Christmas, I'd fly on a magic carpet!"

Bob never forgot the lengths Tibbetts would go to for his men, but he often wondered how Tibbetts convinced General Wolfe that the repair had to be done in Atlanta. Could there have been a wink and a nod on the general's part as well?

Throughout his life, Bob felt that the atomic mission, officially designated Special Bombing Mission No. 13, was justified. For awhile afterwards, he received a lot of appreciation letters. Especially thankful were veterans who served on Okinawa preparing for a land invasion of Japan. However, when I knew Bob, it was post-Viet Nam, and people were beginning to question everything connected with the country's military history.

Bob did not feel comfortable speaking in public about the atomic mission. Consequently, an entire generation of students was deprived of an eye-witness account of a very important event. Shortly before he died, however, Bob did co-author a book titled *Fire of a Thousand Suns.*

That was also the time when Bob and the other crew members felt very disappointed by some of the decisions made by the National Air and Space Museum in Washington on how the Enola Gay would be displayed, and how the mission would be interpreted to the public.

It was a time when things had completely changed in the world, and the bad guys were now on our side, also wearing the white hats. The former Axis nations had become America's closest friends.

The crew of the atomic mission had apparently become an official embarrassment to the government they had so faithfully served in time of war. Bob (possibly the other surviving crew members as well) felt cast aside by the bureaucrats. I don't believe he ever got over his disappointment with those who were so quick to revise history into a politically correct version.

However, nothing ever stopped Bob from attending reunions with pilot Paul Tibbetts and the other surviving members of the atomic crew. I still remember the day I received a color photo of Bob standing with the others at a reunion in — of all places — Japan.

I appreciated all that Bob did for my son Gary, including sending him the home addresses of the other crew members. Gary wrote to them all, and every one of them promptly wrote back with their autographs for his collection. They were a great group of guys.

Was the atomic mission necessary? According to Bob, "They (the Japanese) would have fought on until the last man, woman and child, with the last rock they had to throw. It was the decisive factor in Japan giving up."

The guys on Okinawa weren't the only ones thankful for the war's abrupt end. Had it not been for the atomic mission, my Dad — an assistant machine-gunner in one of Patton's 4th Armored Division tanks — fully expected Japan would be his next stop.

He also has no use for those who would revise history a half a century after the fact.

Bob Caron

XVI

The Marine Ace

Many years later, when Gary and I were making documentary films, we discovered another interesting World War II veteran. He made it into the history books as the only marine to become a combat air ace in two different wars. His name was John Bolt.

John, who preferred to be called Jack, lived about 12 miles from us in New Smyrna Beach, Florida. We contacted him late one fall and asked if he would be willing to share his war-time experiences with us on film. He readily agreed.

I will always remember Jack Bolt with a great deal of affection. He was a very thoughtful person who followed up on the phone call by sending Gary two autographed photos and an autographed biographical background. Even though I had not met him in person, I knew I would really like Jack Bolt.

Our agreement was that we would get together for the taping session after the Christmas holidays. Unfortunately, it was not meant to be. Shortly after our telephone conversation, Jack's health went into a serious decline. On the next phone call, he was barely able to talk. Shortly after that, he died.

Some of the people who have had a story to share with us, unfortunately, did not make it to the big screen. Jack Bolt was one of them. I will always remember Jack for his kindness and generosity toward my son. We will forever cherish his autographed photos, and it is only fitting that we at least tell his story in print. Jack Bolt was a true American hero.

Jack was born in South Carolina in 1921. In 1941, approximately six months before the attack on Pearl Harbor, he enlisted in the Navy, underwent flight training and emerged as a second lieutenant in the United States Marine Corps.

In 1943, Jack Bolt was assigned to the South Pacific. Initially, he was in a fighter pilot pool established to replace combat losses from the Guadalcanal invasion: VMF 214, commanded by Gregory "Pappy" Boyington. Pappy would go on to win the Congressional Medal of Honor.

The squadron thought briefly of naming themselves 'Boyington's Bastards,' but soon settled on the name 'Black Sheep.'

On July 23, 1943, Jack was engaged in a dogfight over Bougainville. He safely emerged from the encounter after shooting down two Japanese Zeroes. The following month, as he was returning to base after escort duty, he spotted three barges laden with enemy troops and cargo.

Single-handedly he attacked all three, destroying two and seriously damaging the third. By the time he returned to base, Admiral Bull Halsey was complimenting him for successfully waging a one man war. Semper Fi. Do or die.

The next day, Jack shot down a third enemy aircraft. He was two kills away from being designated an ace.

By December 23, Jack Bolt was a Marine captain based within striking distance of Raboul, New Britain. At the time, Raboul was a major center of enemy activity. On that day, as Americans on the home front prepared to celebrate Christmas, Jack Bolt shot down two more enemy aircraft and became a World War II ace.

On January 4, he celebrated the new year by shooting down two more Japanese planes. When the unit was disbanded shortly afterwards, he had already qualified for two Distinguished Flying Crosses.

To me, what really made Jack Bolt's story unique was the fact that he went on to become a combat pilot with jet fighters in the Korean War. There, he shot down enough enemy MIGs to be designated an ace a second time. To this day, John Bolt is in the history books as the only Marine pilot to be designated an air ace in two different wars. It is a feat that will probably never be matched again.

In my mind, I can't think of anyone more deserving of a Congressional Medal of Honor. While we can never share this heroic story on film, we are privileged to include Lt Col. John F. Bolt, USMC in the *Flight of the Blue Heron*, and we are proud to dedicate this segment of the book to his wife Dottie and his son Robert.

As I said before, Jack Bolt was a true American hero.

XVII

Courtney's Story

Though we travel the world to find the beautiful, we must carry it with us, or we find it not.

Ralph Waldo Emerson

In 1999, a 17 year old local high school student named Courtney Rice took sick on a Saturday and was dead by Monday. As one of her friends said, "Young people aren't supposed to go into the hospital sick and not come out."

When my son Gary graduated from high school in 2003, he received an award for his participation in the performing arts. It was named after a girl he had never heard of before. Two years later, however, Gary knew plenty about Courtney Rice. He decided he wanted to somehow share her story. We talked it over and developed the idea of doing a documentary film.

In talking with Courtney's mother Shirley, Gary found a person deeply committed to getting the word out about the link between aspirin, viral infections, and the deadly condition known as Reye's Syndrome. We agreed that the best way to reach a film audience was through film festivals. So I set up a small film company to get things rolling. It was the birth of Blue Heron International Pictures.

Reye's Syndrome killed Shirley Rice's daughter. Shirley, however, could not accept the possibility that her beautiful and talented daughter might have died in vain. Consequently, she sought ways of getting information out to parents about the signs and symptoms of Reye's Syndrome, as well as the importance of an early diagnosis.

In the film, she warns about the products which can trigger Reye's — products commonly found in our medicine cabinets — products such as aspirin.

The Blue Heron film project spread Shirley Rice's message far and wide. In doing so, we hoped that other young lives might be saved. Reye's Syndrome is a killer that strikes suddenly, and it is relentless.

Within a day of entering the hospital, Courtney's brain had swollen beyond what her skull could hold. She was beyond hope almost before anyone in the hospital could even figure out what was happening.

Turning over to us hundreds of family photos and videos was emotionally painful for Shirley and her husband. However, both parents realized that getting the message about Reye's out to parents could save others from the type of heartache they were enduring.

In the film, a doctor and pharmacist provide vital information about Reye's Syndrome. The most poignant moments are those which feature the beautiful and talented Courtney. They are truly the most powerful elements of the film. We see Courtney from the time she was an infant in her parent's arms to her days as a maturing young woman about to drive her first car. We are in tears, because we already know how this story will end.

The details of Courtney's short life speak directly to the heart of the audience, far more than the medical information which the film provides. The production screened at two film festivals, capturing a "Best Documentary Filmmaker" award. It has been used in hospital in-service training for nurses, and was broadcast via satellite television in Oslo, Norway.

Blue Heron International Pictures was off to a great start. Not only did we have a film which gave us immense satisfaction, we also knew that we were potentially helping to save lives.

As one of her friends says in the film, "If Courtney's story helps save but one young life, her legacy will be one of great love."

Courtney

XVIII

Courier of Peace

This is the way of peace. Overcome evil with good, falsehood with truth, and hatred with love.

Peace Pilgrim

Within a year of releasing *Courtney*, Blue Heron International Pictures was going strong, and we had just completed our third production, *Eyewitness To History*. The film told the story of a teenager who — by a quirk of fate — ended up in the bunker with Hitler during the last days of the Third Reich.

In 1933, the world's most prolific mass murderer in recorded history came to power in Germany. With his doctrine of hate, Adolf Hitler injected political poison into the minds of every child living in The Third Reich. Armin Lehmann was one of them.

Armin's mythic journey began with a descent into the hell of world war. At 16 years old, Armin had experienced bloody combat on the Eastern Front, and he had sustained serious wounds. Yet his Fuehrer demanded more of this boy-soldier.

Armin's journey to the deepest recesses of hell was complete when he entered the Fuehrer's bunker to become one of Hitler's last couriers. In our film, *Eyewitness To History*, Armin tells his story.

"I was selected by Reichsjugendfuehrer Artur Axmann to be a member of a *Hitler Jugend Helden* (Hitler Youth Heroes) delegation to visit the Fuehrer in Berlin on his birthday. I met Adolf Hitler in the Reich Chancellery garden (also known as the *Hinterhof* or backyard) outside his bunker on his last birthday, April 20, 1945. I became one of his last couriers as a member of Axmann's staff.

During my duty as a courier inside and outside the bunker, I witnessed the total collapse of the Third Reich. I was able to observe the final days of Hitler, Eva Braun, Martin Bormann, and Joseph Goebbels and his family. I was in the adjacent Party Chancellery when Hitler committed suicide.

After Hitler's death, I participated in the bloody breakout from the bunker. It was the night of May 1. Dr. Gertrud asked if the Goebbels children were dead yet, but no one knew. Borman was still drunk, and I heard Major Weltzin tell Axmann that he wouldn't take Bormann along in that condition. General Wilhelm Mohnke (commandant of Hitler's bunker) had also refused to take Bormann.

Mohnke's group was to be the first to leave the bunker. We were broken up into 20 small groups for the break-out, each of which would exit after a short interval. I was in Axmann's group, which was fifth in line to leave. Axmann became impatient, however, so we were bumped up to third in line. He had no intention of taking Bormann either.

As I was about to exit, someone gave me one of two suitcases to carry. Each one was stuffed with a half million Reichsmarks in cash. The garage area was crowded with

Mohnke's elite SS troops, so our group waited in a storage area below the Chancellery. Then it was our turn to exit the bunker.

As Axmann, Weltzin and I approached Weidendamm Bridge, all hell broke loose. A deadly rain of bullets and shrapnel poured down on us. Thick choking smoke, explosions, and flying sparks added to this night from hell. I thought then of my own death. I comforted myself with the thought that — even if my body were torn apart — my soul was bullet-proof and would remain whole."

Armin

XIX

Armin Becomes a Peacemaker

Blessed are the peacemakers.

The Bible

Within minutes, Axmann traded the suitcase Armin was carrying for a letter which he ordered Armin to try to deliver to Grand Admiral Karl Doenitz. Doenitz was in Flensburg, and now in charge of the crumbling Third Reich. Hitler had designated him as the next Fuehrer.

Armin never made it out of the firestorm. Hit by shrapnel and possibly buried beneath the rubble of a collapsing building, Armin was eventually dug out by German 'rubble women.' Mercifully, while he lay unconscious, they removed anything that connected him with the bunker. This kind act by strangers would save him from a Soviet gulag, and allow him to reach the American Occupation Zone two months later.

Mythic journeys end on an uplifting note, and so it was with Armin. In 1938, when Armin Lehmann was a child of ten, he was required by law to join the Hitler Youth. At ten years old, he admired the uniform, and he eagerly looked forward to the adventure ahead.

Armin has always been a gentle soul who often expressed his love of animals and people through his poetry. He recalled many beloved childhood pets, ranging from dogs to a faithful deer living in the forest near his home. He also recalled a loving, nurturing mother, and a very strict father devoted to the Nazi cause.

Armin's poetic soul never embraced the teachings instilled into the members of the Hitler Youth. Nor did he ever embrace the beliefs of his father. A life-long barrier of the heart and mind would separate the two for life.

Armin recalled one particular day as a Hitler Youth. An elderly woman, visually impaired and wearing an armband with the Star of David , was attempting to cross a busy street. He assisted her to the other side.

A group of older Hitler Youth riding by on bicycles spotted this random act of kindness. They stopped, got off their bikes, and administered a serious thrashing to the boy. His father was more concerned that his son had helped a Jew, rather than the fact that he came home beaten up.

Armin continued to disappoint his father by failing to display the level of fanaticism required for admission to Nazi leadership schools. His gentle soul would not fit in to the doctrine of hate — another disappointment to his father.

It is an irony of history that one of the least fanatical children in the Third Reich would end up as Hitler's last courier — in the bunker with the Fuehrer right to the end. It is even more ironic that such a person would totally renounce his Fuehrer and Nazism several months after the war ended.

Yet at 17 years old, upon learning of the Holocaust, that is exactly what Armin Lehmann did. His decision caused a life-long rift between father and son.

Once he learned of the genocide perpetrated by Hitler and his henchmen, Armin's moral compass led him away from the Fuehrer he so faithfully served.

Totally rejecting Adolf Hitler and the Nazis, Armin chose to build a new belief system in which he could work for a better world. Armin Lehmann became a peacemaker. He would travel to more than 150 countries, delivering his message of compassion and understanding to all who would listen.

Armin's story has also been told in two autobiographical books, *Hitler's Last Courier* and *Inside The Bunker*. His story is an incredible one, a story about a compassionate person and his epic journey to hell and back. Armin's hope has always been that future generations will learn from the mistakes of the past.

More than anyone else, Armin Lehmann has been the guiding light behind the Blue Heron films. His message of compassion, tolerance and understanding — both toward people and animals — became our message.

Audiences around the world have watched our animal films and our Holocaust documentaries. They were all made based on the values and principles we learned from Armin.

From the responses we have received regarding our films from around the globe, we have no doubt that hearts and minds have been opened by our message — one that Armin so patiently and lovingly taught us through his words and his actions.

In October, 2008, Armin Dieter Lehmann transitioned from life at the age of 80. His last days were spent in dignity, with the satisfaction of knowing that a new generation of people throughout the planet was hearing about tolerance, compassion, and non-violence.

XX

Claire Goes into Hiding

When we feel love and kindness toward others, it not only
makes others feel loved and cared for, but it helps us also
to develop inner happiness and peace.

Dalai Lama

One of the people we heard from in response to the film about Armin was married to a school-teacher in South Carolina. She had invited a Holocaust survivor to speak to her students and had recorded the presentation. The couple sent me a DVD, asking if we could do a film based on the survivor's experiences.

At the time, we had no plans to develop such a documentary, and filed the DVD away. Some months later, I decided it might make an interesting film project.

I contacted the survivor and her family in South Carolina, but ran into a major snag. Whenever documentary film-makers do a story, they must secure releases from people, consenting to use their images and interviews in the film and in any promotional material connected with the film. The Holocaust survivor consulted with family members who advised her not to sign any consents. The project fell apart.

By this time, I was committed to the idea of a Holocaust documentary, however. So I asked an acquaintance in the Daytona Beach area if we had any

Holocaust survivors living nearby. Two of the most amazing women I have ever known walked into my life at this point, and all of our lives were never the same after that.

Claire Soria was only five years old when her parents gave her up to Christian neighbors in Brussels, Belgium. I often think of Claire's story as the Anne Frank story with a happier ending. No ending can be totally joyful when one's parents and other family members are murdered, but the joy comes from the fact that Claire survived the Holocaust, emerging from hiding at the end of the war.

Her story, like all eyewitness accounts, is best told in her own words.

"My name is Claire Soria and I was five years old when the war started. My dad was a tailor who ran a workshop where they sewed beautiful dresses and coats. I attended kindergarten, played with the school children, and enjoyed going to school.

On weekends, we would go to the park with my cousins and my Aunt Dora. Sometimes, we would walk through the woods. We enjoyed listening to music on the record player, and everyone listened to the news on the radio.

When I was six years old, my dad gave me a sewing basket. He wrote inside, "To my daughter, Clara, on her 6th birthday, Your dad, Nathan." My mother put pictures of her family in Poland in the sewing box, as well as pictures we took of our family.

We had a balcony where we lived, and we enjoyed watching parades. Then one day, I remember going out on the balcony and seeing and hearing the thumping of endless rows of German soldiers marching down the street. They were followed by tanks. At that moment, my world changed.

My family was told to sew a Jewish star on their clothing. Soon afterwards, I was forbidden to attend school. My parents went into hiding with my Aunt Dora and Uncle Bert. I was left with our neighbors, a wonderful Christian family who risked their lives by hiding me.

Lambert and Lea Sabaux changed my name to Yvette, and told everyone that I was their grandchild. They tried to send me to another school, but the principal warned them that if I happened to be Jewish, I would surely be taken away. So Lambert and Lea picked me up at lunch-time, and for the next four years, I did not attend school.

By this time, Jewish people were called terrible names. It didn't make sense why this hatred was directed toward us. I started to feel ashamed to be Jewish.

My parents still tried to visit me when they felt it was safe. However, the Gestapo discovered where my mother and Aunt Dora were hiding, and arrested them. Soon after, my dad was told to get off a bus he was riding, and he was arrested as well. My parents were taken to Auschwitz, where they lost their lives. When I was told my parents were deported, I could not stop crying.

By then, people were getting arrested all the time. The Gestapo were arresting not just Jewish people, but anyone who tried to hide them as well. During their raids, I was often sent away to stay with other people willing to hide me at great risk to their lives. Everyone did what they had to do. When they felt it was safe, I returned home to my Christian family.

The Allies started bombing the railroads and bridges. Towards the end of the war, the German army bombed the same areas to keep arms, food, and supplies from reaching their destination. We would hear the sirens and find a place to hide. Some people went into shelters; others went down to their cellars. We could hear the bombs, as they destroyed homes in the neighborhood. Soon, food became scarce. We were told that the German troops had to be fed first.

After the war, I kept praying that my parents would survive and would return, but it was not meant to be. They were among the six million innocent people who were brutally murdered in concentration camps during the Holocaust.

The people who saved my life wanted me to stay with them, but they were taken to court, and I was told I had to move away. I felt so alone. I loved these wonderful people who had risked their lives to save mine. I didn't want to leave them….."

Today, Claire Soria gives children piano lessons out of her home. During her long days in hiding, when she was unable to attend school, Lea Sabaux taught her how to play the piano. The legacy of this heroic Holocaust rescuer and her husband lives on today —through Claire Soria's piano lessons.

Claire with her father's last birthday gift

XXI

Safe Haven at the Warsaw Zoo

You are a child of the universe, no less than the trees and the stars. You have a right to be here.

Desiderata

When Blue Heron International Pictures decided to do a story about a heroic zookeeper in Warsaw who successfully hid 300 Jews from the Gestapo, we never dreamed that we would find a Holocaust survivor who went into hiding at the zoo.

Yet, against all odds, our producer in Israel, Alex Ringer, found a man whose boyhood memories did indeed include hiding at the Warsaw Zoo. It was only one portion of an incredible story — a story that can soften the hardest of hearts.

Moshe Kenigswain Tirosh vividly remembers his childhood in Warsaw, Poland during the Holocaust.

"I was born in 1937. We lived in Warsaw on Vilenska Street. We were a middle class family. My father had a large carpentry shop, and in addition to that, he was a boxer and even represented Poland on the Polish National Boxing Team.

What I remember from that period of time, is that the war started in September, 1939 when I was two-and-a-half years old. In October, the Germans had already evacuated us from our homes into the Ghetto. I saw a

89

swarm of people with suitcases, and I saw that my father and mother were very sad. That really saddened me too.

So my father, mother, and younger sister went to a place which later became the Warsaw Ghetto. They put us into an apartment in 91 Novolicki Street — an ugly house, unlike ours. I was always crying because I felt something very bad was happening. I didn't know exactly what was happening.

In the Ghetto, life was more or less just going on. Really it was 'less' than 'more.' There was a supply of food and water. The Ghetto was very densely populated, however. The streets were filled with people, and the apartments were filled with people. People were everywhere — lying in hallways, entrances to buildings — everywhere.

I began to feel hungry, and I kept crying to my mother, saying "I'm hungry, I'm hungry." The Germans had stopped the supply of food into the Ghetto. We had no water apart from one or two hours a day...I don't know.

There were sights of horror — people looking like skeletons just lying in the streets. Men on wagons would come around all the time, and pick the dead bodies up by the hands and feet. They would throw them on top of the wagons. All these things are engraved in my memory.

I remember one episode when we didn't have anything to eat in our home. We did have a lot of money, because my father was financially stable.

So my mother took me and went to the town market, and this is engraved deeply in my mind. In a dark corner of the market, she found a woman who sold her a quarter loaf of bread. The bread was hard as a stone. My mother said to me, "Take this and chew on it slowly."

When I brought the bread to my mouth, I noticed in front of me sat an old man like my grandfather, with eyes 'popping out.' I could see that his lips were eating the bread together with me.

So I gave the bread to this old man, and my mother yelled at me. I told her, "Look at this grandfather. He is hungry." This is one episode I remember well.

Things just got worse in the Ghetto..... diseases broke out, mainly typhus. Most of the Ghetto was bed-ridden with sickness. We also got typhus, and my father was the one who had it the worst — probably because he was used to working the hardest and this sickness just paralyzed him.

My mother said she needed to do something. So she put on a pair of trousers, which wasn't acceptable back then, and at night she climbed over the wall to the Polish side, trying to find food. In one of the neighborhoods, a few young men ganged up on her, and started to shout, "Jewish woman, Jewish woman."

She began running from them, and out of one of the alleyways came a 19 year old guy. His name was Zigmunt Pientak, and he shouted to the guys who were chasing her, "Leave her alone. She is not Jewish. She lives here."

He said to my mother, "What are you doing?" She said, "I don't care about anything, I need to get food." So this Zigmunt Pientak, 19 years old, went to his mother, who worked in the market, and came back with potatoes and cabbages. He gave them to my mother, and then he saw her safely back to the Ghetto.

My mother told Zigmunt where we were living, and that my father was one of the champion boxers. He was very impressed because it was a big thing back then. Believe me, even today, it will impress Polish people.

Zigmunt Pientak promised that he would come to the Ghetto and bring us food. And so he did. He would always bring potatoes and cabbage. I think this was how we were saved from the typhus. There was no hygiene, but at least there was food.

The Ghetto began to prepare for rebellion. As a child I started to notice how everything became secret and quiet. People whispered among themselves. And so I understood that something was happening. I didn't know exactly what. I could tell from the atmosphere that something was happening. My father was very serious. He would disappear for awhile and then come back.

One day, my father called me. He opened up my coat, tied something around my waist, and closed up my coat. He told me, "Moshe, go over to the other side. 'Uncle' will give you a candy, but don't stop on the way." I so believed in my father that I went without hesitation and didn't stop.

'Uncle' opened up my coat, took something from my waist, and put something else on me. He said, "Go to your father." This would happen a few times a day. My mother would shout at my father, "What are you doing? Why are you putting the child in danger?" He told her, "Quiet. Everyone is participating."

Zigmunt Pientak tells about one day when he came to bring us food. My father said to him, "You need to bring weapons — a pistol or a rifle." Zigmunt said, "It would be hard to bring a rifle. How would I walk with it?" My Father replied, "So bring a pistol."

Zigmunt bought the gun with money my father gave him, and brought it to the Ghetto. In one of the meetings with Zigmunt, my father said, "Zigmunt, look for a family that could receive us on the Polish side. I will pay whatever is needed."

My brother Shmuel was born in 1942 under the floor. People who were hiding with us wanted to kill him — to strangle him — because he was crying. My mother didn't have milk, and so all she gave him was a wet cloth. She didn't sleep, and she said to my father, "I must move him to the Polish side."

Shmuel wasn't circumcised, so they wrote a note to put with him, with the name Stanislav Pomorski. That night, my mother went over the wall. Zigmunt was waiting for her on the other side. They put my baby brother in a cushion, and placed him at the corner of the street. Then they waited and watched.

In the morning, a Polish policeman came by and saw the child. While they were standing to the side, the policeman asked Zigmunt and my mother, "Whose child is this?" No one answered. So the policeman brought the child to the Orphan's Home for babies. They received him there, and that was that. My mother came back to us. My mom, Regina Kenigswain, gave him a safe place — a safe haven — in order to save him.

Zigmunt came back one day and said that there was a family living on Karankova Street, which was exactly in front of the Ghetto on the Polish side. He said that for a certain amount of money, they were willing to receive us. My father said, "Okay, we will pay whatever is needed."

At night, they put Stefcha, my sister who is two years younger than me, and myself into a sack. We were together with another six bags containing some junkyard stuff. Zigmunt managed to get a type of prumantka — a cart and horse. My mother and father went over the wall in the dark of night, and we traveled to Karankova Street."

(After a few weeks, the Polish landlady began to fear for her life and ordered Moshe's family out of the house where they were staying).

"The Germans would kill the whole family without asking many questions, if they found that you were helping the Jews.

Now, in the middle of Warsaw, in the most difficult time, we didn't know what to do. My father said to my mother, "Let's try the Zoo." We had great connections with the Zoo through Grandpa Sobol. He would sell fruits and vegetables to the Zoo.

Once again, Zigmunt Pientak assisted us. His mission was to hire a 'Roshka.' A 'Roshka' is a kind of carriage with a hood. No one wanted to drive us. Finally, someone agreed for a good sum of money, but on the condition that Zigmunt would sit at the driver's side. We approached Kirveza Bridge, over the Wisla River. Bridges were strategic places guarded by the Germans.

At the bridge, a German came out and shouted, "Halt!" Father anticipated this and told Zigmunt to pour some vodka on the horse and the carriage. It was getting dark and it had started to rain. The German smelled the vodka and said, "Polish pigs, go away!" He took us for drunks and let us pass. The same thing happened on the other side of the bridge, and we finally reached the zoo.

Antonina Zabinska, who was the wife of Jan Zabinski, the zookeeper, received me and my sister. This was in October or November of 1942. I remember that it was raining all the time. So the Zabinskis brought me and my sister Stefcha to the basement of their villa. They gave my mother and father pieces of fur and allowed them to stay in the animal cages.

I don't remember much from our time there, but I do remember when Antonina started to wash and scrub our heads with a chemical that would make us look Aryan. She used bleach in order to dye our heads blonde. However, she scrubbed too much, and we ended up with red hair. Then someone said that we came out looking like squirrels, and this became our undercover name. We were the squirrels.

We didn't stay at the zoo for long. The Zabinskis had a maid who was very anti-Semitic, and didn't want the Jews to be helped. So there was always a danger that she would deliver us to the Germans. Later on, I found out that there was a big rescue operation going on at the zoo involving hundreds of people. At the time, however, I thought we were the only ones hiding there.

I remember Ryszard Zabinski (son of the heroic zookeepers). He was four or five years older then me. In 1942, I was about five years old, so he must have been about ten years old. He and his mom, Antonina, would bring us our food. We would look horrible because we always suffered from hunger. We never went outside. We knew very well what it meant to be 'underground,' and we realized we had to be quiet because of the danger. I understood it very well by then.

We would just stay in the basement the whole time. We sat there quietly, and we didn't make any noise. We didn't cry. Nothing! We didn't play, but passed the time sleeping instead. It was all very serious."

Moshe (Photo by Alex Ringer)

XXII

A Reign of Terror

Nothing is worth more than this day.

Goethe

Asia Doliner was a Holocaust survivor who appeared in both of the Holocaust films released by Blue Heron International Pictures. She was truly an amazing woman who survived the Warsaw Ghetto, the liquidation of the Ghetto, the Warsaw Uprising, two concentration camps, and a German slave labor munitions factory.

Asia was 17 years old when Hitler invaded Poland. "When the Germans arrived, a reign of terror began," said Asia. That reign of terror is best documented in Asia's own words.

"My name is Asia Doliner. I was born in Stanislav which is in southeast Poland. Our family consisted of my father, mother, and I had two older sisters. When the war broke out, it was September 1, 1939. At that time I was 17 years old. And it came unexpectedly. The Germans made a secret pact with the Soviet Union, and they divided Poland. The western part went to Germany. The eastern part went to the Soviets.

We had a beautiful big villa. They kicked us out of the villa. Luckily, we had a cottage in the back. So that's where we lived. The Soviets were there until June, 1941. Suddenly, around June 20, 1941, the Germans broke that pact. They attacked, and the Soviet army started to retreat to their borders. Then the Germans occupied Poland.

The minute the Germans entered, it was a reign of terror.

The first thing they did, they arrested professionals: doctors, lawyers, teachers, professors, rabbis, clergymen. When you say 'arrested,' you expect to be called to court and so on. Witnesses and so on. That wasn't the case. If you were arrested by the Gestapo, you were just as good as dead. That's it. You never saw those people again.

One day, my sister and I came back from the quarry to our little cottage, because we never went back to our villa, not under the Germans. As we entered our little house, we saw Gestapo SS men. They were in the process of arresting my father. We begged them, but nothing doing. They took him away. Immediately, our family and friends came running. They saw what happened and said, "You must leave the house, because we are surprised they didn't arrest you too. They usually take the whole family."

So we just grabbed our coats and handbags, whatever little money we happened to have. We ran away early in the morning. We had a cousin who had a farm 25 km up in the mountains.

We arrived at our cousins' farm. They received us with open arms, and they said it was very quiet there. They didn't see any Germans. It was very quiet, and they had lots of food. It was wonderful for a few days.

One day, we were sitting and eating lunch. In Europe, you eat the big meal at lunch. Suddenly, we heard screams and cries. Children were running and crying. We did not know what was happening. The Ukrainian peasants…they initiated a pogrom. They were running after men, women and children — with hatchets — killing them.

So we ran out — my sister, my step-mother and I. We did not know where. We ran to a hayloft, which was one story high. It was in a barn. We got up in the loft and we were hiding there. Meanwhile, children were crying, "Momma. Momma,"……and then it was quiet. They killed everybody. And we were thinking, "What are we going to do? How will we get out of that place?"

The three women sneak away during the night. The next day, Asia's stepmother is discovered and immediately executed. Asia and her sister make their way to the city, where her oldest sister and baby are living in the ghetto.

"We were smuggled into the ghetto. For the first few days we were very happy because we were reunited with our sister. It was a one room thing, but we were happy to be together. However, life in the ghetto was just awful. Miserable!

The SS would come day or night, pull you out of your rooms, and either shoot you right on the spot, or deport you. So we were told that if we got jobs — important jobs outside the ghetto — then we would not be deported.

So we scrambled to get jobs. My sister got a job with another group of women cleaning apartments for German families *(Occupation troops and officials brought their families with them)*. I got a job on the Gestapo Wirtschafthall — a Gestapo farm. It was on the outskirts of the city.

At 6 in the morning, the SS would come to the ghetto gate and pick us up — the whole group. We were over 100 people consisting of young women and young men. The SS would march us to work. We had to wear the armbands with the Star of David. We could not walk on the sidewalks because we were considered sub-humans.

They worked us very hard. It was a back-breaking job in the fields, lasting a whole day. We had very little food. They would give us watery soup and a ration of bread, and that was it.

One day, as I was coming home, I approached the ghetto gate. My older sister was standing there. I saw her eyes were swollen from crying. I knew something terrible had happened. Sure enough, my middle sister — as she was coming back to the ghetto gate — had been arrested and taken away. So this was a horrible thing, but the next day I had to go to work. We cried all night.

We went to work the next day. The gardener was a Polish guy and he liked me. He said to me, "You know, Ashka, there's an officer — a Gestapo officer — whose birthday is today. I want you to take over a bouquet of flowers to him." The Gestapo courtyard was just across the street.

The gardener picked me and a friend of mine to walk over there and deliver the flowers. He told us the name, and we knew that Gestapo officer because they were around us all the time.

I went over and gave the officer the flowers. He was so appreciative and thanked me. "Danke schoen. Danke schoen," he kept saying.

As we were starting to go back, we were near the Gestapo offices and a big field. My friend looked and said, "Oh my God. Look at that. There's your sister Duschka. The whole group — they are turned to the wall. They are waiting for execution."

When I saw that, I ran back to the same officer, who only minutes before I had given the flowers. I said to him, "Please. Please. You see that girl in the trench-coat with the stripes? That is my sister. Please let her go."

He drew a gun and said, "If you don't run away, I'll shoot you like a dog." I ran away, and this was the worst day of my life because I hated myself. I should have let them kill me.

When I came home to the ghetto, I told my sister what happened, and she said, "How naive can you be? You begged a Nazi for mercy? He would have killed you. He wouldn't have let her go, and I would have lost you both."

After that, our life was not the same. We were terribly depressed. I had to go back to work, and my sister had to take care of the little baby. Whatever little bread I got, I always saved it to take home for the baby.

One day, the SS didn't take us home. They didn't march us back to the ghetto. Instead, they put us up in a barracks, and we did not know why. We imagined that something must be going on in the ghetto. Sure enough, after three or four days, they took us back to the ghetto.

As we entered the ghetto gates, the first thing we saw were members of the Judenrat — the Jewish Council appointed by the Gestapo. They were hanging from lamp-posts.

When I got to our little apartment, the lock was broken. I went in. Whatever little food we had — like dried peas or beans — was spilled on the floor. Everywhere there was broken glass, broken dishes. There was no sign of my sister or the baby, and nobody around to ask.

Finally a neighbor came in. She said she was hiding. She didn't know where her children were. They were teenagers. She was hiding because, when an Aktion comes like that, it comes suddenly. Everybody runs in a different direction.

So that night I couldn't cry. I could *not* cry, but I was very angry. I set out to do anything in my power to run away. I talked to a girl who worked with me on the Gestapo farm and we both decided to run away. She was originally from Warsaw and older than me. She said, "I will run away with you — together."

She kept on saying to me, "We have time. The later we go, the better it will be, because it will be closer to the end of the war." This made sense, but what we did not know was that the SS planned to liquidate the ghetto. Once again, they put us in barracks while they conducted an Aktion. They told us to take a few things from the ghetto. We took our belongings, and that's it. No more ghetto.

The SS kept us alive because they needed us to work in their hothouses and in the fields. One night, I woke up and I saw lights, SS men, and some women getting dressed. I said to another friend, "Tilja, what is going on?"

Tilja said, "Thank God, they didn't call our names. Go back to sleep." That's what she said, but how can you go back to sleep? The SS men told those women that they were needed for an urgent job somewhere else.

I pretended to sleep, and the doomed women got dressed and were taken away. In the morning, we found out they were all killed.

One morning, we came to work and people asked, "Did you know? Did you know that Phillip disappeared?" Phillip was a guy who worked on the farm also. The men were in different barracks. During the night, he disappeared. So I said, "Good for him."

Phillip had told me one evening after work that he had a mother, a brother, and a sister in Warsaw. They were all living under assumed names. I said, "How come you are still here?" He replied, "Well, I just didn't go when I should have gone, and now it's too late." Then he disappeared. We said, "Wonderful!"

After I came back to the barracks from work at 6, a girl came running up. She said, "You know, there's a Polish woman. She's looking for you."

I said, "For me?" She said, "Yes. She insists. She has a letter for you." She took me over to that woman, and I looked at the note. I read it ten times. I couldn't make sense of it. It was very simple, but I just couldn't believe it. It was a letter from that Phillip.

His brother sent somebody from Warsaw. He had Polish friends from the other side of the ghetto wall — Christians. There were people who worked on the Gestapo farm, but they didn't work as slave workers like us. They were paid workers who came in the morning and went back home in the evening. They had special permits.

The woman handing me the letter was such a worker. It was a letter from Phillip. It said simply, "If you want to run away to Warsaw, follow this lady's instructions, and do what she tells you — and don't tell anybody *anything*!"

The woman told me, "Go to your barracks. Pick the nicest dress you have. If you have lipstick, put on lipstick. Comb your hair nicely, and wear nice shoes — and don't tell anybody anything!"

In the barracks, all 20 women were sitting on their bunk beds. I went over to my suitcase and I took out a black dress. I put it on. I put on silk stockings and shoes with heels. They looked at me as if I were crazy. Nobody said a word. They didn't ask me anything.

After I put on lipstick, I asked myself, "How can I walk out? We have been so close. We have become so close under such conditions. I cannot walk out like that." So I told them, "I want to tell you something. I have a chance to run away. I know that it is 99.9% sure that I won't succeed, but I have to take the chance."

They said to me, "Go! May God be with you. We here have no chance. We are doomed. If you have the *slightest* chance, go."

We had to pass by SS men at the gate. They would be looking for documents which indicated we were Christian workers going home. Naturally, I took off my armband. I didn't wear my armband, but I had it in my fist. Most of the SS men knew me, because when I worked at the hot house, they would come in to warm their hands.

I said, "You know. I look different. I look like a human being." As I was approaching the gate, the woman gave me a little work permit to show to the SS men.

About ten feet from the SS men, the gardener's helper saw me, and he was confused. He said in Ukrainian, "What are you doing?" I said, "Stay well, Michael," and kept on going. Had he motioned or pointed a finger at me to the SS, I wouldn't be here today to tell the story.

We passed by the SS men and reached the outside of the gate, where another lady was waiting — a Polish lady. She went in and got my suitcase and walked back out. Then we started to walk.

When we got to a street where there were civilians, I relaxed a little more. I was still not sure that they weren't taking me to a police station or the Gestapo, but then I came into a courtyard and heard Phillip's voice.

The friend who was supposed to run away with me originally had told Philip about my situation before he escaped from the farm. She felt so bad because I wanted to run away sooner, and she said no. She felt guilty. Phillip listened, remembered, and came back for me. I didn't know him very well, but he was a hero to me."

Soon after her escape from the Gestapo farm, Asia assumed the identity of a Polish Catholic, and found a job as a maid near the Warsaw Ghetto.

"It was Easter. It coincided with our Passover. The family that I worked for had a little child. The family went to church that Sunday, and then they all came back home. They all went out on the balcony. One child — a boy about 12 years old — said to his grandmother, "Grandmother, Grandmother. Look at the Jews, how they are burning!"

And he was laughing.

The grandmother said to that child, "This is not a laughing matter. They are Jews, but they are also human beings. We don't know what is waiting for *us.*"

This was so prophetic. In the summer of 1944, the Poles initiated an uprising and we started to build barricades.

The Germans were still very powerful. They had planes. They started to bomb. They flattened the old city where I lived. There was hardly anything left. We were running for three or four weeks from one shelter to another. For a month, we had no water and very little food. Who would give you food? You had no soap. You had nowhere to wash. Nothing! We were like rats, always running.

At the last shelter where we holed up, we heard the Germans. They said, "If there is anybody in there, you come out with your hands up. Otherwise we will throw in hand-grenades, and you will all be killed."

So we all came out and they immediately deported all the young people to Germany. I was among them. They put us in cattle cars. That's how I arrived at the concentration camps. I came as a Pole, however, not as a Jew. Conditions were very bad, but for Jewish people in the same camps, conditions were 100 times worse.

We were taken to Flossenburg, then Ravensbruecke. We waited outside the camps, and finally they ordered us in. Then they took away everything — even glasses I had worn since I was five years old. They even took my false Kennkarte (German identification card) that was so important to always carry around.

They gave us some thin clothes — patched so that we would not run away. How could you run away? The people could easily spot you and know you were from a concentration camp.

We were issued wooden shoes. No underwear. No stockings. We used to stand for roll call for hours and hours.

One time, it happened to be a nice day. It was very cold, but it wasn't raining. A German doctor was sitting in the courtyard — a young doctor — and he picked young women out. We had to strip completely, and we had to run around the doctor. We didn't know what this was all about. It turned out to be a selection, and I was selected.

If you had a little pimple or whatever, you went to the other side. We did not know at the time what it all meant. Those who had a perfect body survived. The others perished. They took us to a munitions factory to work — a building in Spandow.

In Spandow, we had to have our hair and bodies checked again. They gave us warmer clothes. As we were marching out, I said to the women nearby, "You know what? I don't know where we are being taken, but it couldn't be a worse hell than this."

Asia worked as a slave laborer in a German munitions factory until the end of the war. When she arrived in Florida with her new husband, she shouted....

"I'm in heaven! I'm in heaven! I'm in heaven!"

XXIII

Israel's Blue Heron

Let the beauty we love be what we do.

Rumi

I've never met Alex Ringer. I've talked to him on the phone, corresponded with him by mail, and communicated with him in more than a thousand e-mails. Yet, Alex has become dear to my heart, and we all consider him a part of our family.

I came across Alex one day when searching for stock photos of the Holocaust. His daughter Sharon had some interesting images posted on the internet, which I thought would add beauty to our first Holocaust documentary, *Deliver Us From Evil*. I sent off a request for permission to use those photos, and received back a torrent of talent and energy which would catapult Blue Heron International Pictures onto the world stage.

Alex Ringer ended up becoming our producer in Israel. He became an incredible source of material for both of our Holocaust documentaries, especially *Safe Haven: The Warsaw Zoo*.

Against all odds, Alex located and interviewed Moshe Kenigswain Tirosh, the Holocaust survivor who spent part of his childhood days hidden at the Warsaw Zoo.

Because of Alex, both of our Holocaust films have been broadcast on network television in Israel. Because of

Alex, both films are part of the educational resources at Yad Vashem Holocaust Memorial in Jerusalem and Ghetto Fighter's Museum in western Galilee.

We have come to know and love Alex, his wife Zmira, son Eli (and his wife Galit), daughter Sharon, and grandchildren Ya'ir and Shir. Alex's brother Adam also holds a special place in our hearts.

Shortly before this book went to press, Adam lost his heroic battle with lung cancer. We featured childhood photos of Alex and Adam together with their beloved pets in our heart-warming animal film, *Bogart & Friends*. The film will always be a memorial to Adam, who loved people and animals as much as we do.

All of us at Blue Heron International Pictures will be eternally grateful for the day Alex Ringer came bounding into our lives. In his words, Alex tells how our marvelous relationship all came about.

"In the autumn of 2006, my daughter traveled to the United States and visited the Holocaust Memorial in Boston. I gave her a special stone from our yard to guard her, and also give her a touch of our home.

Reaching the SHOAH stone monument in Boston, she felt an urge to lay the stone there in memory of the six million Jewish people who did not have the chance to return home after World War 2.

I was very touched by her gesture, and told her I would have done the same. After all, her great-grandparents — both from my mother's side (Marcus Family from

Tarnow) and my father's side (Ringer from Krakow) — were murdered in the Holocaust by the Nazis.

My parents were wise enough to leave Europe in the mid-1930's and settle in Israel (Palestine then). They fought the Nazis as volunteers. My father was a mechanical engineer. He joined the British Navy, and served in Alexandria as an officer. He participated in a number of combat operations against the Germans.

As you can see, stories of Jewish families are always bonded together, and the stories told in *Deliver Us From Evil* and *Safe Haven: The Warsaw Zoo* are really special ones."

When Alex said that stories of Jewish families are always special and always bonded together, he wasn't kidding. As we conducted our research for *Safe Haven*, we came across the book, *Refuge In Hell*. Author Daniel B. Silver tells the incredible story of one of the most unlikely safe havens protecting Jews during the Holocaust — a Jewish hospital operating openly in Hitler's capital city of Berlin. Klaus Zwilsky was one of twenty survivors interviewed for the book.

Klaus recalls working as a youngster in the hospital garden, raising vegetables for food. He was not allowed to attend school, or even leave the hospital grounds. Under constant threat of deportation to a death camp, Klaus and his parents miraculously managed to survive the war in Berlin's Jewish hospital — the Krankenhaus Der Juedischen Gemeinde on Iranischestrasse — in the very heart of The Third Reich. Klaus was the person who provided me with the perfect quotation for *Safe Haven: The Warsaw Zoo*:

"I don't want the story to be forgotten, and it needs to be repeated, and people should know about it, and that it really happened. There was such a thing as the Holocaust and it should be remembered."

Emerging from his safe haven in the Jewish hospital after the war, Klaus was the first person to celebrate a bar mitzvah in Berlin.

Our Holocaust films have brought us in contact with some truly incredible people.

We love them all.

XXIV

The Zookeeper's Son

Non-cooperation with evil is a sacred duty.

Mahatma Gandhi

Ryszard Zabinski is a very special person in my mind. So are his sister and his parents. After Gary's first Holocaust film, *Deliver Us From Evil*, was released, people began contacting us with names of others who had survived one of the worst mass murders in recorded history. When we came across the story of the people at the Warsaw Zoo, we knew we had to make a second Holocaust film.

Jan Zabinski was the zookeeper at the Warsaw Zoo beginning in the 1930's. He lived in a villa on zoo grounds with his wife, Antonina and young son, Ryszard. In the closing days of the war, his daughter Teresa was born, making the Zabinskis a family of four.

When Hitler invaded Poland, Jan became a member of the Polish underground. At first, he allowed the zoo to be used to store weapons for the Resistance. Later, he hid far more precious contraband — 300 Jewish men, women, and children. All but two survived the war, and none were ever discovered or arrested at the zoo.

Years later, when he was asked why he endangered himself and put his own family at risk as well, Jan Zabinski stated simply, "It was the right thing to do."

113

Young Ryszard knew the dangers involved in hiding Jews at the zoo. Yet, he never uttered a careless word, and faithfully exercised his responsibilities in the operation. Among his chores was the carrying of food to the special 'guests,' all of whom were named after animals.

War is cruel and takes its toll on both humans and animals. Like Armin Lehmann, Ryszard had a special love for the animals. As a young child, he experienced the loss of his beloved zoo animals and most of his pets. It was the special kind of heartbreak only children can experience when faced with the loss of a little creature they have nurtured and loved.

According to the Dalai Lama, who I have quoted several times already, "To care for anyone else enough to make their problems one's own, is ever the beginning of one's real ethical development." There is no question that Ryszard's ethical development occurred at a very young age. Not many pre-teenaged youngsters can claim to have saved a life. Fewer still can claim a part in saving 300 lives while at grave risk to themselves. However, Ryszard is in this select fraternity of mankind.

So, Gary and I felt it important to tell the story of the heroism at the zoo from Ryszard's perspective. Our film, *Safe Haven:The Warsaw Zoo*, instantly struck a chord with teachers and children from around the world.

The Global Dreamers in Israel featured the story on their website, spreading the message of compassion and 'doing the right thing' throughout the world. One student in Warsaw, Indiana was quite surprised to find it was not a story about his local zoo, but rather a story of a brave family in Poland. Letters poured in from classrooms in Israel, Poland, and even New Delhi, India.

Ryszard grew up to be a civil engineer in Poland. Today, he lives on a pension in a small apartment in Warsaw. As he spreads his family photos out on a table, it is clear to see that his love of his parents and pride in what they did are still strong emotions today. He is a gentle, modest person — the kind who naturally loved and cared for animals, as well as for people. While we think of him as a hero, he prefers to keep the spotlight on his heroic parents instead.

We could not have told Ryszard's inspirational story without the help of another compassionate person in Warsaw. We came to know Feliks Pastusiak, our producer, from a contact provided by Alex Ringer in Israel. Alex just happened to be related to Feliks.

So while one producer chased down Ryszard's story in Warsaw, the other one located Moshe Tirosh in Israel. What are the odds of locating a Holocaust survivor who went into hiding as a child at the Warsaw Zoo? Alex beat the odds, and found Feliks for us as well.

It turned out that Feliks was a god-send. He was working full-time as a producer in Warsaw, so he knew what we as filmmakers would need. It gets better. Feliks also had some major Hollywood credits to his name. He worked as a production assistant to Steven Spielberg in *Schindler's List*. As if that weren't enough to qualify him to work on a Holocaust film, he also worked on Roman Polanski's *The Pianist*, and an action film called *Proof of Life*, starring Russell Crowe and Meg Ryan.

We owe a huge debt of gratitude to Feliks for all that he did for us as producer of *Safe Haven*. In addition to locating Ryszard Zabinski, Feliks also attracted some of Europe's finest talent to participate in the project, including acclaimed photographer, Piotr Bujnowicz.

Because of Feliks, our film is playing in Polish at the very place where the story happened. At Blue Heron, we can think of no finer tribute to the heroic family of zookeepers, than to show their story at their former home - The Warsaw Zoo.

Like Alex, Feliks turned out to be a man of great compassion and a kind heart. He went to great lengths to always make Ryszard feel comfortable throughout the film-making process. We made a number of revisions to our script based on what Ryszard told Feliks. We wanted Ryszard to be especially happy with our film as a tribute to his parents. We asked Feliks to always look out for Ryszard's best interests throughout the project, and he did so admirably.

I only wish Ryszard and Feliks could have seen the tears of joy steaming down my face, when I learned *Safe Haven* would be screening for visitors at the Warsaw Zoo — the very safe haven which spared 300 precious lives during World War II.

In June, 2009, we issued the following press release announcing this electrifying development.

Safe Haven To Screen At The Warsaw Zoo

The latest Holocaust documentary from Blue Heron International Pictures has become a blockbuster hit around the world since its release last March.

"More than seven million people from around the globe have watched it on the Internet Movie Data Base (IMDB.com), as well as on network television in Israel," said executive producer Richard Lester. "We have had e-mail pouring in from teachers and students ranging from Warsaw, Indiana to New Delhi, India."

Now comes word that has thrilled the Daytona Beach film-makers even more.

"Our producer in Warsaw, Feliks Pastusiak, has arranged for a Polish language version to be screened daily at the Warsaw Zoo," exclaimed Gary Lester, the film's award-winning director. "I can't think of a more appropriate place for people to see it, than the place where the events actually took place."

According to Feliks Pastusiak, well-known Polish voice-over artist Jacek Brzostynski will record the Polish version of the narration. "He is one of the best," said Pastusiak. "He is happy to be a part of this film and the tribute to its heroes."

Pastusiak was also responsible for signing on Piotr Bujnowicz as the film's Director of Photography. Bujnowicz is considered one of the best photographers in Europe.

Safe Haven tells the story of heroic zookeeper Jan Zabinski and his family, who successfully hid 300 Jewish men, women, and children from the Gestapo during Word War II. When asked after the war why he took such risks to himself and his family, Zabinski replied, "It was the right thing to do."

"I am very happy that Jan's children, Ryszard and Teresa, are still alive to learn of this huge honor," said Gary Lester. "Imagine them returning to their childhood home at the zoo and watching a film about their heroic parents, right where the entire story took place."

In addition to Ryszard Zabinski, the film also features Holocaust survivors Asia Doliner and Moshe Kenigswain Tirosh.

Safe Haven: The Warsaw Zoo had its world premiere at the West Hollywood International Film Festival in August 2009, and is an official selection at the Route 66 Film Festival in Springfield, Illinois, and the Treasure Coast International Film Festival in Port St Lucie, Florida.

What phenomenal people!

Yet the story that follows tells about another phenomenal person — an elementary school teacher in Israel who found a way to share our film with students throughout the world!

Ryszard (Photo by Piotr Bujnowicz)

XXV

Global Dreamers

Marsha Goren loves her work. For almost 25 years, Marsha has been teaching English as a second language to her fourth, fifth and sixth-grade elementary students. As this book goes to press, Marsha will be preparing for a fresh batch of eager and enthusiastic kids at Ein Ganim Elementary School in Petach Tikva, Israel.

Marsha's mom, Sonia Frenkel, was a Holocaust survivor of Midanjek and Auschwitz. Before passing away in 1991, she asked her daughter "to educate kids for a better tomorrow around the world."

Marsha has created an internationally acclaimed website called Global Dreamers, which is a powerful fulfillment of her mother's last wishes.

"Global Dreamers inspires children to take a deeper look at the world by exploring, exchanging ideas, and using research tools. It supports a positive learning environment and a shared learning experience," says Marsha.

"Above all, Global Dreamers attempts to create a more tolerant individual in a multicultural society. We believe that by understanding and learning about others, children can face a better world."

At Blue Heron, we were very favorably impressed with the children in Global Dreamers. It was obvious to us that these kids are serious about pursuing their goal of making this small planet of ours a better place for all of us. We will always be grateful to Miki Goldwasser, our friend in Israel, who brought Marsha and the Global Dreamers to our attention.

When Marsha agreed to be the educational outreach coordinator for our *Safe Haven* documentary, we had no idea that her level of enthusiasm and energy on our behalf would be astronomical. Once Marsha joined the project, e-mails began flooding into our Port Orange studios. Teachers and students from Poland, Belgium, Israel, and the United States — Global Dreamers from around the world — were telling us how deeply the film had affected them.

A teacher in Poland published a Polish study guide. A student in New Delhi, India created a Power Point presentation. Students in Israel designed website banners. Children's art work flowed in from the United States and Israel. It was simply unbelievable. Our company webmaster spent more than 40 hours putting some of the beautiful and poignant mail up on our website.

Within four months of its release, *Safe Haven* was streaming into classrooms around the world, with website indicators showing three million viewers. That total grows weekly. There is no doubt in my mind that Marsha and her Global Dreamers are having a tremendous impact on the world of tomorrow.

I am reminded of a Hebrew phrase that I believe best sums up this remarkable woman's labor of love — *Tikkun Olam*. It means 'repairing the world.' For the repair work Marsha continues to do, I dedicate this chapter to Sonia Frenkel, the mom who inspired Marsha's dream.

XXVI

Walking in Beauty

God made all the creatures and gave them our love and our fear. To give sign, we and they are His children, one family here.

Robert Browning

At Blue Heron, we believe that animals, like humans, were also created by God, and therefore have a divine purpose on this earth. Armin Lehmann told me that his maternal grandmother would frequently take him to church. There, she would tell him, "Einen lieben Gott haben wir alle." ("We all have a loving God.")

Armin's grandmother also believed that the universe was populated with angels who would do no harm, and even animals could claim God as their own.

In the last year of his life, when Armin was struggling with a stage of dementia that made it difficult to focus on — or remember — events from the previous week, he told me about his early childhood days living in a German forest. "My memory is spotty," Armin wrote on July 7, 2008, "and I am still searching for many explanations. My daily walk recalls things."

That day, Armin thought back to childhood days, and built a picture in his mind of the Lehmann Family — parents, grandparents, and beloved animals. He recalled the names of all of them. There were Treff and Troll, the

English retrievers; Sonja, the Irish setter; and Das Reh, a pet deer who wondered out of the forest into the backyard one day.

While his father wanted Armin to become an ardent Nazi, his mother and grandmother sought to nurture his gentle side. They hoped he would be like the angels who walk among us, and do no harm. The women would be the ones to eventually win over Armin's heart and mind.

For the rest of his life, Armin could find little in common with his unrepentant father.

At Blue Heron, we are committed to the idea that our main responsibility as humans is to encourage patience, compassion, and understanding — among ourselves, as well as our fellow earthlings. There is no place on this earth for cruelty, wanton destruction, or neglect. All life has a purpose, and that purpose needs to be recognized and respected.

In the words of Ralph Waldo Emerson, "Though we travel the world over to find the beautiful, we must carry it with us, or we find it not."

Most of the people I have included in *The Flight of the Blue Heron* have discovered beauty in life. They have accomplished what the Navajo also hope to achieve in their lives — to walk in beauty.

Armin

XXVII

Fuzzy Little People

If you have men who will exclude any of God's creatures from the shelter of compassion and pity, you will have men who will deal likewise with their fellow men.

St. Francis of Assisi

On Sunday, March 2, 2008, we posted the following article on our website. It breaks my heart to this day. Our fuzzy little people deserve so much better. It was titled, *A Death In the Neighborhood.*

Four years ago, while on our daily walk through the neighborhood, we came upon a lost little black kitten. She obviously had strayed from her home and could not find her way back. As lost kittens sometimes do, she attached herself to us and followed us home.

We made a bed for her on the screened porch, gave her some food and water, and left a message at the phone number listed on her collar. Later that day, a little girl, looking greatly relieved, came for the kitten and gave the lost little animal a ride home in the basket on her bike.

Throughout the years, we frequently came across this precious little cat, who always remembered us and greeted us with a meow and frequent roll-overs. We worried about her being loose, especially in a gated community which does not allow animals to run loose.

Things took a turn for the worst this past year, and the little cat began to show signs of neglect. A neighbor put a bowl of water out on the front porch for her. We carried a sandwich bag of dried cat food to put down for her on our daily walks.

Last month, the little cat looked like she might be suffering from mange. With sad and heavy hearts, we continued to carry food on our walks, and discussed contacting the local humane society. Last week, when we discovered that the owners had removed the little cat's blue collar and tags, we knew with certainty that the loveable little creature had become one of the thousands of unwanted and abandoned pets in this country.

Calls went out to the humane society to pick the little cat up. They came out and made two attempts, the last one just two days ago. Unfortunately, they were unable to locate the animal.

Today we found her lying dead at the side of the entrance to our gated community. She had been hit by a car. She managed to drag herself to the side of the road, and lay down on her injured side to die. Sadly, we took a plastic container and blanket, and picked her up.

Once again, for the last time, this unwanted little animal was being returned to the humane society. A small plaque will be placed there with the date she was adopted, the date she died, and a new name: *Angel Wings*.

This beautiful little pet was full of love for humans, but in the end, humans let her down.

Until one has loved an animal, a part of one's soul remains un-awakened.

Anatole France

XXVIII

Charlie and Dottie

Love and compassion are necessities, not luxuries. Without them, humanity cannot survive

Dalai Lama

Charlie Carlson is Florida's most famous folklore story-teller and historian. Charlie has written a number of books, including the iconic *Weird Florida* and a fictional thriller, *Ashley's Shadow*. His books about the paranormal have generated excitement among sci-fi fans around the world.

In addition to being an accomplished stage magician with his own side show, (*Charlie Carlson's World of the Weird and Wacky*), Charlie is also a veteran radio performer and film actor. He is still seen occasionally on cable television in his debut film role as Professor Morehouse in *Curse of the Blair Witch*.

We first met Charlie when we were putting together a paranormal documentary called *The Cleansing*. Charlie came along with a medium to check out a house where some bizarre things were happening. He went on to produce our first blockbuster feature film, *Henry Blackhart is Dead*.

Charlie's most recent assignment from Blue Heron was as an associate producer for *Safe Haven: The*

Warsaw Zoo. Perhaps most important of all, Charlie Carlson loves people, animals, and the environment.

I think Charlie and Gary are fabulous onstage when they perform magic together. Charlie is one of those genuine human beings who knows how to bring joy into the lives of others. I have never heard him say an unkind word, never seen him angry or impatient. He is a creative genius on top of all of that. As far as I am concerned, Charlie Carlson is much more than a producer at Blue Heron. He is part of our family.

Charlie's wife, Dottie, was also a very special person. Throughout the years, audiences enjoyed her portrayal of a hoodoo lady at various venues across the state of Florida. Dottie — appearing under her stage name of Dot Diehl — brought the character to life on the screen, with her memorable performance in *Henry Blackhart is Dead*.

Four months after the release of the film, we lost Dottie to lung cancer. We loved Dottie. She was such a friend to many of the little creatures who came her way.

How many people would stand in the way of a bulldozer poised to bury a nest of live gopher tortoises? Dottie did.

Dottie also rescued and rehabilitated injured squirrels — more than 1,500 of them — and cared for a variety of animals, including a cat named OC and a dog named Miss Scarlet.

Dottie Carlson was only 60 when she left us, but in the short time she was with us, she made our small planet a better place on which to live.

Miss Scarlet and Charlie

XXIX

Starring Miss Scarlet

Mankind's true moral test consists of its attitudes toward those who are at its mercy — animals.

Milan Kundera

In addition to filming compelling stories of human triumph against all odds, our company has also delighted in bringing animal stories to the screen as well. Our first documentary of this nature, *Fuzzy Little People*, tells of the plight of shelter animals across the country, while encouraging pet owners to be responsible with their special friends.

At this time, I am personally acquainted with only one very famous animal — a dog who has her own press agent. I have included a recent press release below which very nicely sums up the world of the newest canine star in America — Miss Scarlet.

"Originally known as Dakota, Miss Scarlet is a seven year old female boxer who was born in Sumter County, Florida. She spent the first year of her life as a neglected pup chained to a tree in someone's backyard. Then came a life-altering event. She was rescued by two animal lovers.

Dakota soon joined the Charlie Carlson family and found her mentor, a large brindle boxer named Bubba

James, from whom she learned her boxer etiquette. Because of her unique reddish coat, she was renamed 'Scarlet.'

In 2007, she made her show business debut on stage in a magic show. In 2008, Miss Scarlet was featured (as a lap dog, named Dolly) in an independent film produced by Blue Heron International Pictures. The film was called *Henry Blackhart is Dead*. For her part in the production, Miss Scarlet was presented the 2008 Blue Heron Animal Choice Award.

In 2009, Miss Scarlet began work as a co-star in the Florida PBS special, *Weird Florida: Roads Less Traveled* — a one hour, weird and wacky travelogue, featuring Charlie Carlson, Florida's Master of the Weird.

In the show, Charlie and Miss Scarlet are on a quest to find the Sunshine State's most unusual places. The show takes viewers from Key West, across the Everglades, and up through Central Florida. The trip ends in West Florida.

During the filming, Miss Scarlet traveled nearly 1500 miles in the Weird-Mobile, most of it with her head stuck out the window and her chops flapping in the breeze.

Miss Scarlet is fond of walks on the beach, pork chops, and running in large circles. She now resides in luxury with her own six cats and a squirrel in New Smyrna Beach, Florida."

The greatness of a nation and its moral progress can be judged by the way its animals are treated.

Mahatma Gandhi

XXX

The Man with the Handlebar Moustache

*Love life, and life will love you back. Love people, and they
will love you back.*

Arthur Rubenstein

Ted V. Mikels is our most recent discovery, and he
fits in nicely with those who have helped make Planet Earth
a better place to live.

Ted is friendly, compassionate, and caring. He loves
making movies, and has engaged in his labor of love for
more than 60 years. Scores of 'wannabe' filmmakers have
come his way, and Ted has taken them all under his wing
and shown them how to practice their craft.

Ted is everyone's friend. He also has a sense of
humor that won't wait. Sit back, relax, and prepare to smile
— as we introduce you to the world of Ted V. Mikels.

We first came across Ted Mikels when Gary bought
a DVD of his classic 1969 movie, *ASTRO ZOMBIES*. One
of the special features on the DVD had Ted offering tidbits
of wisdom to those who wanted to make films.

In that special feature, Ted encouraged his audience
of aspiring film-makers to treat people right. He told about
lining up a warehouse as a location for one of his films, and
informing the owner that he had no expectation of being
able to pay anything for it. The owner had no problem with
the arrangement, and Ted filmed his scenes at that location.

139

Later, when the film became a commercial success, Ted went back to the surprised owner and paid him for the use of his warehouse.

I told Gary that here was an example of an honest man — a film-maker with true integrity. Gary contacted Ted, offered to donate artwork for promo cards for Ted's current project (*ASTRO ZOMBIES M3 Cloned*), and a new and beautiful friendship developed.

We have since learned that for more than 60 years, Ted has taken under his wing everyone aspiring to learn the craft of making movies. Even the casting notice on his website for his current production assures aspiring actors and actresses that they will have something to do in the production, if they just show up. In other words, no one will be turned down. Everyone with a serious interest will be able to proceed one step closer to realizing their dream of being in — or making — movies. Ted was making dreams come true.

Ted is one of my favorite senior citizens, and he has definitely enriched the independent film landscape, as well as the lives of all who have been involved with his projects over the past half century. I am proud to be able to say that my son Gary, also an aspiring filmmaker, has worked with Ted Mikels. Ted's story is definitely worthy of notice by the folks at Blue Heron.

As a child, Ted enjoyed photography. He even learned how to develop his own pictures in the family bathtub. By 15, he was also performing before live audiences on stage. During his younger days, Ted could boast of being an accomplished magician, performing with the Amazing Mandrake.

In addition, Ted performed as a ventriloquist (with a dummy given to him by Mandrake); a musician (accordion and bongo drums); and a fire-eater and acrobat. It wasn't long before he made his way to Hollywood as a stuntman. Before leaving the carnival circuit, however, Ted worked as a barker for Sealo (The Seal Boy), who bonded with him and loved his company.

Ted has been making movies for more than sixty years, and he has no plans to retire. "I may slow down, however, at age 104," chuckles the 80 year old horror classic icon, who tells interviewers that his films are "baloney sandwiches with no cheese, a little bit of mustard, and a lot of heart and soul."

Mikels made films in almost every genre possible, including a paranormal movie, *Blood Orgy of the She-Devils*. "It's a campy little witchcraft film," said Ted. In order to write a believable script for the film, he studied paranormal investigation techniques first. He is best known, however, for his cult classic horror films.

Starting out in movies as a Hollywood stuntman, Ted had no idea that he would one day be creating trend-setting zombies. He was having too much fun shooting flaming arrows at a fort defended by Kirk Douglas *in Indian Fighter*. Ted remembers shooting "most of the flaming arrows in that picture. In fact, I shot the flaming arrows that just missed Kirk Douglas and hit the flag poles, setting the wagons on fire."

In one scene, director Andre de Toth had Ted shooting flaming arrows at the fort from a galloping horse. Since he was left-handed, he naturally maneuvered his horse around to the left to shoot. "I had no idea the director had sent another group of Indians galloping up on my left," said Ted laughing. "I spun right into them, went flying, hit the ground with running horse hooves all around me. The shot is still visible in the movie."

Many of Ted's fans are unaware of the fact that he was an accomplished archer at the time, which is probably why studio executives trusted him to shoot an arrow narrowly missing Kirk Douglas. Ted also created the blend of tar, pitch and kerosene which allowed the arrows to continue flaming well after striking their target.

Four years later, Ed Wood, known as Hollywood's cheapest filmmaker, turned out *Plan 9 from Outer Space,* complete with a cast composed of neighbors, his girl friend, and his dentist. Despite cardboard tombstones that tend to fall over in the graveyard scenes, Wood successfully introduced actress Maila Nurmi (Vampira) to film audiences at the dawn of the 1960's, and created a campy cult horror classic which still attracts audiences fifty years later.

Zombies were also on Ted Mikels' mind. "I do know that I created my "*ASTRO ZOMBIES*" in 1960. I had never heard of such a being, but I gave my new super-human beings the name that has become synonymous with mine. I know of no zombie movies filmed in color before that. Mine were to be the super-humans sent into early space exploration. Wayne Rodgers (co-producer) talked me into making it campy."

Lack of financing delayed Ted's project for nine years, however, allowing George Romero to bring his zombies to the screen first. In his film *Night of the Living Dead*, seven people attempt to survive the night in a rural Pennsylvania farmhouse, as legions of the undead drop by.

By this time, Ted Mikels was also working as a Hollywood producer and director, no longer shooting flaming arrows and accidentally falling off horses. He knew that his turn had come to offer up some of his own creepy undead for the horror fans, and he finally had the financing to do it.

In 1969, *ASTRO-ZOMBIES* appeared on movie theater and drive-in screens, and the world hasn't been the same since. Audiences were treated to 91 minutes of Ted Mikels' zombies intermixed in a wacky way with foreign spies, CIA agents, beautiful women, and a mad scientist — all in full color!

Of his $37,000 budget, Ted used $3,000 to attract John Carradine for the starring role. "He was an absolute joy to have on the set," recalls Ted. "It was indeed my pleasure to work with John Carradine, as we had been involved in four projects together. We bonded well. He asked me while we were shooting *ASTRO ZOMBIES* if I had any parts for his son, as he wished to get into making movies."

Ted didn't have a part for Carradine's son, but he did hire aging screen legend Wendell Corey as Carradine's co-star.

According to Mikels, "Wendell Corey was so very professional working on the shoot. Ten years earlier, I had unknowingly filmed him standing by his Marlin catch in Mazatlan, Mexico, so we had a lot to talk about. Both Mr. Carradine and Mr. Corey absolutely were totally professional, knowing their lines in detail before appearing on my set."

It was left to Corey's character, CIA Agent Holman, to describe the undead creatures to thrill-seeking audiences. According to Agent Holman, they had a "synthetic, electrically driven heart, a stainless steel mesh stomach, a plastic pancreas, and a cellulite liver."

Interestingly, one future Hollywood celebrity had his *ASTRO ZOMBIES* scene end up on the cutting room floor. Actor Peter Falk would always be remembered by television fans as the rumpled detective, Columbo, but his humor was too much for the zombie world.

"Peter Falk was so funny that I had to cut him out of the movie. His natural humor brought an element into the scene that was supposed to be very serious, so I couldn't use his footage. You would laugh when you were supposed to be alarmed, and that did not work. Also, I did not have the time to totally explain the scenario to him. So to be fair, it was not his fault," Ted explained.

Looking back over forty years of making horror films, Ted Mikels concludes, "I guess there are *ASTRO ZOMBIES* fans everywhere in the world, and no-one has attempted to participate in my realm of these monster killing machines. I'm appreciative of that. Everyone has

gory, bloody zombies, but no-one except Ted V. Mikels has
ASTRO ZOMBIES!"

Ted is an American original. Gary will always
treasure his association with Ted, working as the graphic
artist and photographer who created the promo cards and
theatrical posters for *ASTRO-ZOMIES M3: Cloned* —
produced and directed by none other than that iconic filmmaker himself — Ted V. Mikels!

Ted

XXXI

Batman's Sidekick

I originally intended to leave one of the most incredible people I have ever met out of this narrative. I had a very practical reason for doing so. Now that I have finished this book, I will begin a collaboration with him to write his autobiography. Why in the world would I reveal his fascinating story in this book, when his own book will be coming out next?

I changed my mind, however, because this work seemed incomplete without him. There seemed to be a hole that needed filling.

Johnny Duncan is a milestone on the flight of the Blue Heron. So he cannot — and will not — be left out of this book. To have his complete story, however, readers will have to wait for publication of Johnny's autobiography. Johnny remembers his childhood days in rural Missouri during the Great Depression (the first one, not the one we're in now). His dad operated a barbershop, and all of the latest news and opinions were probably expressed and analyzed over a haircut and a shave.

Johnny never appeared in a Blue Heron film, yet he is truly part of our effort to make our world a better place. We invited Johnny and his lovely wife Susan to join us in Daytona Beach, where the Blue Heron would honor him for a Lifetime Achievement in Film Award.

Johnny started his movie career in the year that some film historians believe was the best ever for Hollywood. In 1939, audiences flocked to theatres to watch Clark Gable and Vivien Leigh in *Gone With The Wind.*

Some may also have seen teenager Johnny Duncan portray a towns-boy that year in *The Arizona Wildcat,* starring Jane Withers and Leo Carrillo.

In 1943, Johnny was cast in his first of several films with Huntz Hall and Leo Gorcey — The East Side Kids. The film was called *Clancy Street Boys*. He soon found himself cast in a scene opposite Humphrey Bogart in the wartime thriller, *Action in the North Atlantic.*

Before he retired from movies and television, Johnny had worked with most of the great stars in Hollywood. In 1949, kids watching the Saturday matinee chapter serials watched Johnny perform as Robert Lowery's sidekick in *Batman & Robin.*

However, his days with the East Side Kids seemed to provide the most recognition among his acting peers. Johnny tells the story of the day he found himself on the television set of *Rawhide*, starring Clint Walker. When Walker spotted Johnny, he went up to him and said, "I know you. You're one of those East Side Kids."

Johnny had been cast in the role of the town troublemaker, along with a new actor also playing a heavy. Walker didn't recognize the other guy. His name was Clint Eastwood, and he was Johnny's ride home that night.

Johnny's exciting tales as a participant in the 'golden age' of Hollywood will all be described in his upcoming autobiography. For our purposes, we need to point out that Johnny is far more than an actor with some great memories of the past. Johnny is also one of those caring and compassionate people who enjoy bringing happiness into the lives of others.

During his personal appearances with us, as the first recipient of our *Lifetime Achievement in Film Award*, Johnny took time with each and every one of his fans. He has a natural ability to make everyone who comes his way feel special. He loves animals, and he loves people. In everything he does or says, Johnny Duncan brings sunshine into people's lives.

We invited an actor to our awards ceremony, but we got much more. We found a true humanitarian whose impact on our small planet has been substantial. Johnny will always be part of the Blue Heron family.

Johnny

XXXII

My Son, Gary

Build me a son, Oh Lord, who will be strong enough to know when he is weak, and brave enough to face himself when he is afraid — one who will be proud and unbending in honest defeat, and humble and gentle in victory.

General Douglas A. MacArthur

I have always enjoyed going on adventures with my son, Gary. When he was around eight years old, I decided to introduce him to the world of the stock market. I bought Gary one share in six different companies of his choice. I was curious to see how a kid his age would invest in the future.

Gary chose Coca Cola, Pepsi, Wrigley's, McDonalds, Marvel, and Time Warner. I was really impressed with his portfolio. Over the years, Marvel went under, but the other stocks grew, split, and grew some more.

It was easy to understand most of his choices. They were soda companies, a chewing gum corporation, a restaurant chain that had served up a billion tasty burgers (and untold billions of fries). They represented companies whose products appealed to kids. But why Time Warner?

The answer turned out to be quite simple.

All of his life, Gary has placed one super-hero above all others in his hierarchy of fictional role models —

151

Batman. As this book goes to press, I believe Gary has enough Batman memorabilia and costumes to open up his own museum. Bruce Wayne, aka Batman, is the one and only — at least as far as Gary is concerned.

So even at the age of eight years old, Gary knew that Warner Brothers was currently the home studio for Batman (Let's not forget, however, that back in 1949 — when Johnny Duncan was playing Robin in *Batman & Robin* — Columbia was the studio that released the first Batman films).

Fifty years later, however, Batman had found a new home at Warner Brothers. So the company that owned Warner Brothers — Time Warner — became Gary's favorite among the six stocks chosen.

I have never shied away from doing something a bit unusual. So it was a foregone conclusion that I would be taking my son to the next Time Warner stockholders' meeting. With his one share of stock in hand, we were off to the company's Burbank Studios.

There is no doubt in my mind that Time Warner had many shareholders who owned more than one share of the company. Nevertheless, I contacted corporate headquarters, told them their youngest stockholder would be coming to the meeting, and booked our airline tickets. It would cost us more to attend the meeting than the cost of Gary's entire stock portfolio, guaranteeing he wouldn't realize a profit on his investment until sometime after the age of 105. However, you must remember — Warner Brothers was home to Batman! A trip to the studios would be priceless.

Most of my adventures are what I call 'low budget spectaculars.' This excursion was no exception. We flew into Burbank on a discount airline. I am not kidding when I say discount airline.

On the way back from Burbank, we got stranded at the airport during our layover in Phoenix. The company couldn't come up with enough pilots to fly all of the planes! (I would later learn that flying was not one of Batman's super powers either).

However, that situation occurred at the end of our adventure. The beginning gets even better. When we arrived in Burbank, we checked in to a motel that had seen its heyday come and go. Nevertheless, it had been a location for several films. The motel was located in a nice, quiet neighborhood, just a couple blocks away from the NBC Burbank studios. A nearby convenience store, looking just like the Quickie Mart in *The Simpsons,* was where we loaded up on snacks for the evening. We ended the night with a pizza delivery. Life was good!

The next morning, we finished off the Twinkies for breakfast and took a cab to the Warner Brothers Studios. Our stockholder pass got us through the main gate. Then we arrived in a courtyard and experienced a sight you will only see in Hollywood. Long tables, laden with all kinds of delicious breakfast foods stretched as far as our eyes could see. White-gloved servers provided everyone with ample quantities of whatever they desired.

Gary and I laughed. We had filled up on Twinkies, not realizing just what type of world we were stepping into. It sure wasn't the world of low budget discounts!

Then an amazing thing happened. Some corporate folks spotted Gary. They had been alerted that the company's youngest stockholder would be present. Within minutes, they were photographing Gary with an assortment of costumed Looney Tunes characters. The photos were Polaroids, and as soon as they were developed, an assistant put them in special Warner Brothers photo display cards. Soon, Gary had a stack of unique souvenirs to take home, compliments of the company he partially owned.

Before he could catch his breath, the young stockholder was ushered into a studio theater to watch the latest movie previews. I remember one of them starred Arnold Schwarzenegger in *Eraser*.

Once the previews were concluded, Gary moved to the lecture hall where the company president would preside over the meeting, but not before he was told that he would get an employee discount on anything he bought at the studio store.

The highlight of the visit occurred when we were seated on a golf cart and given a VIP tour of the Warner Brothers back lot. We motored down the street where I recalled seeing a marching band playing 76 Trombones in *The Music Man*. Before long, we were on the set of *Little House On The Prairie*. Trust me. If a movie was made at Warner Brothers Studios, we were on that set. We saw them all on our drive through the back lot.

During our break for lunch, we happened to be on a 'hot' set where Steven Segal was filming *The Glimmer Man*. We didn't see Steven, but one of the scariest-looking movie bad guys brushed by us on a mad dash to the rest room. It was the first time we ever came that close to a homicidal maniac, wearing a spiked bracelet on his wrist and a pistol in a shoulder holster. He was running right toward us! Thank goodness it was on a Warner Brothers movie set. Steven Segal, by the way, was nowhere to be seen.

Over the years, there was one thing that Gary learned from his dad. Don't be afraid to ask. It worked for me in getting to meet the Beatles, and it got us the star treatment at Warner Brothers. Gary had certainly gotten his money's worth out of his one share of stock. (Did I mention that the corporate report that year carried a color photo of Batman on the cover?)

Gary has always had to struggle in school. He has had to overcome a learning disability called dyslexia, in order to be able to successfully read and write. People who have Gary's type of dyslexia see things in their minds as pictures, not words. True dyslexics tend to be highly creative, talented, and gifted — especially with hands-on types of activities.

Gary, for example, was only seven or eight years old when he tore apart his mom's broken vacuum cleaner, fixed it, and put it back together again. Back then, he also wired my entire home theater surround sound system, just by looking at a diagram. To this day, he fixes anything that breaks down in our house.

Gary loves art, music, and drama. It was no surprise to see him major in photography in college, and now motion picture production in graduate school. Gary shares the same disability with such other creative artists as inventor Thomas Edison, actor Tom Cruise, and child actor Jon Provost, who played Timmy on the *Lassie* TV series.

While dyslexia impacts both reading and written language skills, Sylvester Stallone started off down the road to fame and fortune — not as an actor — but as a dyslexic screenwriter! The script he wrote — *Rocky* — was so powerful that the studios would have it at any cost, including casting him in the lead role.

Rocky is an unforgettable story of a guy who struggles against all of life's obstacles to achieve his dream. Dyslexics know what it is like to struggle to reach their dream. Stallone was writing from the heart.

When Gary was in elementary school, we came across another dyslexic person who had reached the height of his profession. He was in town to speak to the graduating class at the local military academy. I told Gary to watch closely. I was betting the speech would be delivered from memory.

Sure enough, it was. There wasn't a note-card to be seen. It was a beautiful speech. Once again, we had taken to letter-writing to alert the speaker to the fact that Gary was struggling to overcome the same obstacles that had blocked his path to success.

When he read the letter, in which Gary called him his hero, tears welled up in the speaker's eyes. When he arrived home at Rancho Mirage, California the next day, Gary's fellow dyslexic pulled out a color photo and a Sharpie, inscribing the following message:

"To Gary Lester, best wishes. Gerald R. Ford."

I believe dyslexia is not a disability, but rather an alternate learning style. It is difficult to refer to some of the most gifted and talented artists, inventors, writers, performers, and thinkers as disabled. Many are also some of the most compassionate and kindest people you ever could meet. I used to say that they have 'teddy bear' personalities.

One thing is sure, however. Most people who are dyslexic know the meaning of struggle and the importance of compassion. It was no accident that Blue Heron would end up making films about people and animals in distress.

Despite his difficulty passing a state standardized test required for a high school diploma, Gary had no trouble earning both an associates and a bachelors degree in photography. He also completed training at The Hollywood Film Institute in Los Angeles, where he earned a certificate of completion as a producer. His film debut as an actor occurred in 2001 when he appeared in *Flamingo Rising* on The Hallmark Hall of Fame. The production aired on CBS television.

At Blue Heron International Pictures, Gary became an award-winning director. His documentary films have screened at film festivals ranging from Boca Raton, Florida to Busan, South Korea, and from warm, sunny Daytona Beach to chilly Ontario, Canada.

Gary's films have won 'Best Documentary' awards, 'Audience Choice' awards, as well as the coveted Crystal Reel from the Florida Motion Picture & Television Association. His latest Holocaust documentary had a world premiere at the West Hollywood International Film

Festival. Several of his films have appeared on cable television, and two have been broadcast nationwide in Israel, subtitled in both Russian and Hebrew.

Gary has also been honored with a director's page on the Internet Movie Data Base (IMDb), where many of his films have been recognized and made available world-wide. As of this writing, more than three million people have watched the trailer to *Safe Haven* on the internet. It is both mind-boggling and humbling at the same time.

When I started the film company, I did so with a very limited objective in mind. I wanted to support my son's first (and I thought only) film at film festivals.

I had totally underestimated my son's ability to tell compelling stories on a movie screen. One project led to another, and it wasn't long before Gary's message of compassion, tolerance, and peace was traveling warp speed around the world to millions of receptive hearts.

The flight of the Blue Heron has been the adventure of a life-time!

Gary

Royal Jubilee (Rm 665)